ENGINE RUNNING

21st CENTURY ESSAYS
David Lazar and Patrick Madden, Series Editors

ENGINE RUNNING

ESSAYS

Cade Mason

MAD CREEK BOOKS, AN IMPRINT OF
THE OHIO STATE UNIVERSITY PRESS
COLUMBUS

Library of Congress Cataloging-in-Publication Data
Names: Mason, Cade, author.
Title: Engine running : essays / Cade Mason.
Other titles: 21st century essays.
Description: Columbus : Mad Creek Books, an imprint of The Ohio State University
    Press, [2022] | Series: 21st century essays | Summary: "A memoir-in-essays about
    one man's childhood in rural West Texas, as he comes of age and grapples with
    masculinity, religion, queer identity, parental divorce, and his family fracturing"—
    Provided by publisher.
Identifiers: LCCN 2022027968 | ISBN 9780814258507 (paperback) | ISBN 0814258506
    (paperback) | ISBN 9780814282441 (ebook) | ISBN 081428244X (ebook)
Subjects: LCSH: Mason, Cade. | Mason, Cade—Childhood and youth. | Mason,
    Cade—Family. | Authors, American—21st century—Biography. | Coming of
    age—Texas, West—Biography. | Texas, West—Biography. Classification: LCC
    PS3613.A8154 Z46 2022 | DDC 814/.6 [B]—dc23/eng/20220815
LC record available at https://lccn.loc.gov/2022027968

Cover design by Charles Brock
Text design by Juliet Williams
Type set in Adobe Garamond Pro

for my parents

CONTENTS

I

EXODUS

One by one, we children slip away from home:
from hallways with bare feet—cold floors—and ears against closed
doors and muted voices on the TV in the living room, we slip into
a trance: the A/C rumbles through the walls of our grandparents'
house, and the house, we think, smells clean, like water: it fills
slowly with the steam uprising like a spirit from the dishwasher,
running—quiet, disturbed—from the half-light of the house's
every afternoon nap, and we listen to our grandma through the
brown door to her bedroom snoring softly to herself like a small
bird in its nest, and her sound, we think, is like a signal: to pry
at, slide the sunroom's glass door open, to run into the great West
Texas summer heat and out, into the backyard: past dented pans
for mudpies three-quarters-buried in her garden and the steady
arch of water from the roving yellow sprinkler in the bold green
grass and the line of untrimmed bushes with red roses that we pick
and place inside our hair, our clothing, we run: beyond the edges
of the yard, we leap over the thick-beam wooden fence, we land,
we plant ourselves in brown-white cotton fields that wait at every

corner of our world for every new day's pair of still-undirtied feet to press a history—evidence, for a moment, of us and our escape— and the trails we leave show how we run: with arms extended, brushing up against the cotton, inside the rows our fathers dug into the earth, until, we have, to catch, our breath—until we, then, exhaust ourselves—until we look to the empty stretch behind us, at what holds the orange-bricked house, the giant white workshop, the old tin barn and older farm equipment—and everything, we think—(one day, we'll think)—is central to nowhere: this place where all our fathers lived as children—the place where we grow up—and we turn our backs to where it is we came from, toward the endless way ahead of us, to nothing but the blue-white sky and open fields and, at their ends, the long dirt roads that aim on, aim off—and we sit below the rows of cotton, hiding—like our escape is threatened—and yelling, and it's a good sound—and we laugh—we run—

until our childhoods, like tiny
imprints, are windswept, clean, away.

KNOWING ME, KNOWING YOU

1. Home, he thinks, is not too far but far enough away: just four, five ABBA songs from town. In these, his family's early days, most days, it's just a mother and her son. She's young—even when she doesn't feel it anymore, only 26. When she walks the aisles of the grocery store, those long-scuffed floors all checkered blue and white, she's often stopped by strangers. Gray and grayer men and women with thin backs bent like question marks, tissues bunched, tight, in wrinkled hands. They tell her that she's beautiful. And she is; and this dying place, they think—Post, Texas, with its highway running through it, and its semitrucks and truckers, its population settled at 4,000—is better for it. The son rides beneath the basket, he's restless, he's impatient, at all the constant stops to talk. And when his mother breaks away, a back wheel of their cart begins to tremor with her push. To squeak along that checkered floor. *It's always these,* his mother says and shakes the cart. Her head. *We always find the broken ones.*

2. In the parking lot, in the car—that white Suburban, streaked and splattered with dried, layered mud the butter color of the fields—his mother reaches for the CD case that's velcroed to the visor. It's a stretch above the passenger seat, and so she leans. She leans until her body blocks the center console. Until: there's a subtle sort of shifting in the air. It's her lotion, caught in the flow. And the air smells—suddenly—*sweet,* smells warm, and then familiar. He watches from the backseat as she slides the CD free. With hands, he thinks, that seem to glow in every swath of feathered light that beams in through the windshield. And in the sun, the CD shimmers too. *Gold: Greatest Hits.* His mother feeds it to the radio. They wait for sound to buffer.

3. He likes Track 3. Her favorite's 11. And still, most days, they start at 1. Disco sounds all right out here. Better than all right: outside, the sky seems almost endless. It rises up in layers, from a light-blonde smear of dust that hovers just above the earth into a nothing-white into a blue that, like the whole of West Texas, stretches deep and boundless. Inside, the car's a constant rattle. Sometimes she rolls the windows down, and all the sound escapes and still embraces them, like some great pressure leaving, fast, and turning back to settle. Wind rushes in and tousles hair, and his mother, in time to the yellow stripes on the road, taps some unseen tambourine against the wheel. She shakes the beat, and he watches. Imitates. *Everything is fine,* she sings, and her voice sounds quiet. Shy and sweet beneath the track. When she catches his gaze in the mirror, she jives. *Ooh, see that girl.* He laughs, and it's something, even then, at 4 years old, that fills the car. She laughs, free, into his rearview stare. *Digging the dancing queen.*

4. And the gray road rises slowly up, and up through oil country. Pumpjacks rock in-place on either side of them like anchored
ships each bound, forever, to a *here*. The car rolls past several jacks
along the sticking asphalt, and some—his favorite—bear long and
wooden donkey ears. They kick, and they drain the land, and, suddenly, the country changes: the rising road spits out to flatness. To
another kind of broken earth. Endless fields of cotton, that sea of
nothing.

5. The son looks beyond his window. Beyond a thousand rows in fields of budding white that dot the dust with empty color. That blur to meet their speed. And beyond all that: there's the great white workshop, that hulking neighbor to the orange-bricked house in contrast—his grandparents' house. The workshop stands alone like some small promise on the horizon, and he sees his mother's looking. At other giants: two bright green tractors crawling in a field nearby. It's a father, a son. Or: this son's grandfather, his father. Or: this mother's husband.

6. Up here, where the land has leveled out, his mother isn't singing anymore. When they pass the dust-blown horse corral of Aunt D and Uncle N. When they pass the cotton gin, its office, where the son goes when his father takes him; where the secretary hands out sugar cubes from the coffee drawer and winks. When they pass the old schoolhouse-turned-community center, what sits faded, yellow-bricked, and empty, with its broken playground in the back, and the Church of Christ across the street—a tiny two-room baptistry—where all his father's family goes and has forever. (A thing that will, in just a few short years, collapse to time and weather.)

7. The son, he sings the words his mother's left abandoned (*I have a dream*) past fenced-in fields of horses, cows, and bales of hay wound tight, and other farms, the neighbors', where another boy his age—a future friend—(*a fantasy*) grows up just down the road inside a house that sits with weather-eaten white walls beneath tall rows of tilting trees that jut up like a fence around the backyard, around the solid blue above-ground pool that settles like relief among the vicious weeds and several scattered, rusted plows—and their car, he thinks, it passes like a bullet from his father's gun to shoot with rising speed (*to help me through reality*) beyond the only world he's ever known and toward the house his parents plan to buy, and somebody, soon, once family grows by one. Where they'll settle—where they'll stay: for the length of this son's childhood.

8. (But just before they get that far, his mother takes a left.)

9. *Sing a new song,* the CD says, his mother hums. She bites at the inside of her cheek. She rolls up all the windows. These days, her hair is short (the only time it may ever be this short), and she works to keep it out of her face. Over ears, behind them. But her movement, again and again, releases it to fall. And the son, he can't know what it is she really feels: when she smiles to the mirror so that her eyes close up to squint—when she catches her own stare and drops that smile. Looks back to the windshield. (And he won't know for years.)

10. When she turns onto the dirt road, their car shakes as if lost. As if it's leaving orbit—or falling, rough, into it. White dust clouds bloom into a blossom behind the wheels that start to slow and then to tremor with her foot pushed light against the peddle. And that white haze hovers in the rearview, and it blots out everything. And it's a memory that the wind soon drives away.

11. *Try once more,* his small voice sings, and his mother looks ahead—and the world out here looks lonely. *Like you did before,* she hums, and the battered farmhouse nears. It's his mother's and his father's. His. And it's surrounded, on almost every side—like some forgotten island—by its cotton fields. Like their distant neighbors' every house, it, too, is eaten-up by wind: the gray paint's stripped in several spots so bare stripes run its surface; a window's cracked from hail; the screened-in back porch bears its holes, with two or three spread open, wide, like exit wounds. There's a thick cement storm cellar buried in the backyard, and the gray tin chicken coop behind it, and the cattle run behind that, farther still. A donkey called Ol' Blue—the almost-color of his name—lumbers, all alone, and toward the gateway of the red corral when he hears his people coming. Three dogs run and join together, bark—and pause, and stare—and bark again, tails wagging. Fat frogs croak in the cattle's trough and leap and splash into it like undug stones the son drops in the water. Beside a line of trees, a long and silver gas tank hisses near the wellhouse by the imprint of a snake's slide in the sand. And the sometimes-call of cattle catches on the wind, a sound of roaming wide throughout the field behind the house: that network of mesquite and sun-drained brush and scattered animal bones. Somewhere close, pushed down beside the aged pecan tree's roots and planted in its hillside, is a splintered wooden door—what the son calls his *trapdoor:* some squarish swinging part left over from that coop his father built. He opens up the door and digs, and *digs,* inside its mouth. He tosses dirt and rock aside to pile up beside it. He thinks he might create a clubhouse. A room, and his, and underground. (Of course, he never gets too far: the ground grows hard against his strength; old roots get in the way.) He digs through afternoons, and his mother watches from the kitchen. The

water that she runs builds steam, and it hides his digging through the window.

12. The white cloud's a wall behind the car and catching up. (The son, he wonders—far away from this life and this world and its home—how his mother must've felt after the radio went silent.)

13. And the radio, he thinks, is hardly ever silent. Not between the two of them—not then. When it's not ABBA's *Greatest Hits,* then it's Celine's, or Bread's, or Buddy Holly's. And the son's small voice, in those early years, is framed inside a twangy lisp. His lyrics blend together, muddy. Understood, with distance. One day, inside the grocery store, it's something that's familiar on the speakers overhead. (Holly's "True Love Ways." A favorite in the car.) The son climbs out from underneath the basket. He tugs his mother at her side, and she looks down from whatever's in her hand. To his arms extended, up. She smiles to that squint and sets whatever on the shelf and lifts him. Holds him to her chest: her hand on his neck: his head against her shoulder, and they sway beside the basket. They dance inside the aisle for the full length of the song—she sings the lyrics in his ear—and baskets pushed by gray and grayer men and women pass without a thought. (When his mother tells this story at several future kitchen tables, she follows it with how he woke one day, and spoke, and that sweet lisp and twang had left him. *My baby,* she says, and lets a weighted breath fall out of her. She smiles, sad. Remembering.)

14. *It was always just you,* his mother says (years later), *and me,* and then she shakes her head—and her hair, longer (now), it falls into her eyes when she looks down: to her hands, settled, clamped together on the kitchen table—*and we were so far out.* One hand frees itself to fix her hair behind her ears before it settles back onto the table, and her other thumb rubs rough into the palm of it. And the son—26, today, like his mother, then—he says he can't imagine. What it's like to be alone most days. In a lonely place. With just a child to talk to. To him, the childhood world was all there is. His father farmed, so he was gone. But he'd always come back home. Covered head-to-toe in dust. With a smile: for him, and for his wife. (The son tries but can't remember his mother's distance from his father—if it started as early as this.)

15. Sometimes his mother's mom will visit. From farther West—
what feels, to him, a world away. With her bright red lips and
bright red fingernails. With hair formed like a dark cloud puff
above her head. She's nothing but vibrant. Nothing but smiles.
The jewelry up and down her wrists, it jangles when she picks him
up and digs her nose into his cheek and sings. And when she sings,
she rocks him in her arms around the living room. The kitchen.
She dances, and he laughs, and so his mother laughs. And the
dust from the surrounding world outside taps code against the
windows. The wind out here is restless: it comes alive and spins
up dust and runs along the earth to rip away what all the fathers
work throughout the year to plow; it marks the land, and marks
the land again, and then again, like an ever-changing mosaic. Like
this world is simply years of dust all pieced together. And it comes
to rest with tight dunes on the windowsills. It howls and falls like
snow inside the chimney. It gathers at the threshold of their home.
And he hears it—almost constantly. Like when he stays inside his
room and plays with Legos on the carpet: when he builds houses,
and destroys them, topples walls, with every crafted dragon's gust;
and when he starts all over. As he puts the pieces back together,
his mother speaks silent in the living room. To her mom, beside
her on the couch. Whose hand is on her back, rubbing. Kneading into her. Until the house sounds like it might collapse—and
the TV plays a familiar tune: a scratchy robotic scream in thirds,
and an extended tone, he thinks, like the sound of the other end
of the phone, and that robot's voice, speaking: *tornado.* And his
mother stands and wipes her cheeks and rushes to his room. Grabs
him. Grabs a blanket, and she holds him to her chest—and he can
feel her wild heart. Can hear the sound outside the windows like a
crowd of something trying to get in. *Hail,* the TV says. His mother

and her mom, they grab for things to hide their heads. To keep them covered from the wind, the *hail*. The *tornado*. And the lights go out, and the TV's screech goes silent, and it's almost like it's nighttime: the world outside the house is dark and only sound. It always happens, his mother must think, so fast. No warning. Her mom's saying *Baby*, first to her between her running, then to him: *Baby*. Her voice is smoothed, free of all the shaking that her jewelry does. When his mother calls him *Baby*, in his ear, the sound is close to breaking. And the house sounds close to breaking. His mother throws the backdoor open, and the screen door beyond that, and the dogs rush in—she calls them back, to follow—and they run out into dark. He looks over his mother's shoulder, to her mom close behind: to red lips and fingernails that vanish when they cross the porch. And the world feels like it's falling—and there's nothing behind them—nothing ahead—and there's the cold touch of rain along their skin, and something hard, small stones—until, he hears the sound beneath the wind of metal creaking—of metal slamming, and wind rushing in to fill the hollow place—where his mother carries him, down, into the earth—and he thinks the underground smells like a lake—and she sets him down, quick. *Baby*, she says, *Hold on*, and runs back up the stairs and screams out to the dogs who rush in, past her, and she screams out to her mom, and they grab the door, they pull it, and the wind, the *hail, tornado*—there's the sound of all its shutting-out, and there's only dark, and there's the cool of the ground below him and the wall against his back, that dirtied water smell and wet mutt-dog. And the world outside the underground beats hard against their cover. He hears their footsteps down the stairs. Smells his mother's lotion, and her mom's, both working hard against the cellar's scent. There's a click beside him—and his eyes adjust to low light. To an outline forming of his mother and her mom, and they're soaked. Standing, wringing clothing. He's dry, he starts to notice, from the blanket he'd been under. Her mom starts to laugh. She runs a hand against her brow. She fixes her hair in ways she can. *Why*, she says, *is it always when I come to town?* His mother sucks in breath, releases it. She digs her palms into her eyes. And he thinks about his father: out there, in a tractor. With a view of the *tornado*. With nowhere to go.

16. For all the time they live out there, they're subject to the wind. They crawl out from the underground to upturned black birds scattered in the yard. To chickens, lying dead. To everything the dogs rush forward to and eat. The trees are stripped of bark or branches tossed around their bases, or they're gone—new gaps in the horizon. The walls of cars are marked with extra dents. And the house: its walls' newest paint is stripped again to the light wood color beneath it; its gray roof's shingles are ripped away and missing; its windows bear new veins. And it seems it's part of this world's never-ending cycle: a building up to great destruction just to start again. Still, somehow, he thinks (at 26), this early world stays standing.

17. The dogs bark, and the loose rock in the driveway sounds its crunching under tires—and the front door of his truck flies open, and it slams. And then his father's at the backdoor, talking to the dogs. There's the sound of their panting. Their running up, their greeting. They jump and lean against his legs so that he has to hold them out. And when, at last, he gets the door closed, he kicks his boots off on the mat and steps into the kitchen. His blue jeans hold yellow-faded tones around his knees; his tan shirt, tucked into those jeans, bulges slight against his belly; the tops of both his white socks stay pure white. Even with the light hair pasted, sweaty, to his brow—even with the boyish cheeks and neck, rough hands, all stained with earth like sloppy watercolors—he's handsome at 28. But his mother—his father seems to know just what he's got in her. The son watches as his father steps over to the sink and wraps his arms around his mother's waist and kisses on her neck. He watches as his father spins her, leans against her, and makes their kiss sound loud so that it hangs for several seconds in the kitchen's memory. *Beautiful,* he calls her. *Hey, beautiful,* he says. He reminds her every time he sees her. And sometimes, it's late in the evening, and there's music playing in the kitchen. His parents do the dishes together. The water steams the window at the sink. And his father starts to sing, and his mother keeps on cleaning. And his father puts a hand against his mother's side and plays it like riff so that she jumps and laughs with both her hands still buried in the sink. He turns her so she's facing him, and she says his name and holds her dripping hands up. Suds cover them past her wrists. She tells him, through a grin, he better cut it out. But he weaves his fingers into hers so that they're pressed together. And she gives in: and he sways her, slow, and holds her side—holds steady—with his other hand. She puts her free hand on his back, and the light tan fabric

of his shirt starts, quick, to darken all around it. The son watches. He laughs. With Lego houses splayed in pieces on the carpet in the living room. With the stuffed bear that he calls Curly leaning in the doorway, watching too. And the soles of both their bare feet press into the cool linoleum, and the water keeps running in the sink, keeps steaming up ghost-touches on the window. His father sings the words into his mother's ear: *And the wonder,* he shakes his head, *of it all,* and they spin, and his mother's laughing, *is that you just don't realize*—and they pause when the music pauses, until it starts back up—and his father catches his mother's eyes—*how much I love you.* And when the song's last note drifts out, she steps back, to the sink, and shuts the water off. The window starts to clear up. The image of the black night starts to show itself. The music's different, changed, then, into something else, and his father steps away, still whistling—her hand's bold outline solid on his back. He watches his mother look down into the water. How she smiles. How that smile turns into a bitten lower lip as she pulls the plug inside the drain: and there's the sound of the music, his father's whistling through the house, and water bubbling in the sink and draining out, escaping.

18. He grows up, just a bit. Just enough so that he sits, then, in the front seat of the car. He's still his mother's passenger, but now he reaches for the case above the seat: for *Gold*. He holds it, careful, at its edges, and he feeds it to the radio. Before the sound can start, his mother, still, she skips it to 11. It's easier, she's always thought, to work the track-list backward. And there's the sound of the CD catching up to itself. And there's the familiar voice: *Tell me what's wrong*, it says. They sing the words to themselves as he looks out through the window. The world that passes fast outside the car remains the same. (He thinks it always will.) And his mother's reflection in the glass is like a phantom on its other side. Her body flies through empty fields and cuts through every tall telephone pole and the small dips in the wiring between them. She nods her head, but just enough so that he barely makes it out. One hand stays still where it grips the wheel, and the other rests to pick quiet at itself, in her lap. The gray road aims on and on, and the windows stay in place so that her phantom self looks trapped in what's outside.

19. Home, he thinks, is not too far but far enough away: ABBA always brings him closer. When every track is like a flash of landscape. Of scattered cells of long-eared pumpjacks and rising canyon walls and utter Western flatness, its horizon. He can close his eyes and see the turns: see the several ridges of the cotton fields: see the yellow-shaded plots of neighbors' land and clouds of dust behind the tractors and the tractors. He can see fathers. His father, in them. And his mother: the radio's familiar dancing queen: *his.* Sometimes, now, alone, he dances to the beat inside his car. In the driver's seat. To that CD of his own. He merges on the highway, rolls his windows down. He turns the sound up just enough so that its voices sit above the wind, above his own voice singing out. And his car speeds like his memory, *knowing.*

THE HOWLING-OUT

The pond's enough for our small boat to float out, aimless, to the middle. It sits on several hundred acres far outside of Post, Texas, and far enough away from where we live to feel like it's a trip. When we're out there—my father and I, with our faces looking over and reflecting off the surface—I might call the pond a *lake*. It's what you do at this age, in the summer between your third- and fourth-grade years. When everything takes on a bigger shape and the heat seems as great as it'll ever be, as it always is, so that you feel no need to claim it. To call it: *heat*. A *problem*. Because you're young, and the heat's just something you were born into.

(And anyway, these things, you think, like heat and boats and camping, never change and never will. It's all a part of living, or it *is* living. Why claim anything?)

My father bought the land off some other, older cotton farmer. Someone creeping toward retirement, willing—or *ready*, in the way, I guess, we have to be, at some point—to give it up. Every time we roll in past the gate, I watch him step out from the truck. He walks to where the fence begins, and each step sinks him lower into what he's worked to plow: that loose soil, dried-up. Upturned. He hooks his thumbs through the beltloops of his jeans and calls out to the expanse with careful repetition: with a nothing-word he's formed, for years, into a chant, and its slowed tones fashion to his drawl. The color of the land appears the quiet pale of wheat. The tree line of mesquite that borders the field stands still as, above us, fat clouds crawl slow against bright blue and cast dark shadows that spread out, ease along, hungry, on the earth. There's no wailing wind today, no birdsong. No passing car or plane or tractor. Just the howling-out of one man, his voice formed by old church hymns: what lifts up, tilts, and sinks into staccato rhythm. He shakes a bag of feed and pellets rush against the plastic, fall on one another like rain. He stares out, like I do, at the edge of field, at the edge of my seat: and the cows, hooked on my father's song, amble through the trees.

In the boat, my father sings a different song. Don Henley. Steve Perry. Roger Waters and *The Wall*. He's like a boy again when the voice of Waters—controlled, *angry*—rises up from a scream to command attention with a drumbeat on the radio. In the truck, on the way to here—this land, his cows, and the pond—my father twists the dial far to the right. He nods to the sound and taps the steering wheel with a thumb. His left hand hangs outside the open window and taps the door, its hail-damaged craters. And the rush of speed furies the hair, much lighter than my own, that hangs wild at his brow. (Today, I think about my father then: how he would grin wide at that open road unfurling up ahead of us like his remembering was a phantom that possessed him.) *Hey!* he yells, with a drawl that's missing in the track. My father looks over to me. *Teacher!* he sings, and narrows his gaze, like he's gearing up to fight. *Leave them kids alone!* And I'm nodding, too, but maybe not enough, because he pulls his hand back in from outside and grips the wheel. He reaches over with the hand that kept the beat inside the truck and taps against my chest. *C'mon, Bubba,* he says, he calls me. *Hold on to this,* he doesn't say but maybe wants to. (*To this version of us,* he'd mean, if he'd only say it.) And he looks back to whatever's on the stretch of road ahead of us. And the radio plays on.

My father doesn't sing the lyrics on the water, but he whistles them. He holds the words behind some inner rift, and still, even in their absence, I hear them. They're the sounds of his youth, and of mine. *His* sounds, instilled in me. Like sparks to fire up some inner protest. (What'll flash, *bright,* as I grow older. Too old, I'll think— behind the radio of my own car one day—to listen to my old man; too far-removed from West Texas heat and boats and camping.)

When the light dies down enough so that we can't make out the water from the land, my father rows us back to shore. We build ourselves a campfire from the fallen branches and the brush we scouted in the daytime, and it sits a lonely distance from the tent my father's pitched. As he sits and pokes the flames to start with a stick, I crouch inside faint light beside the moon-shape on the water. I grab a nearby wooden oar, and I extend it: I reach across reflected dark and tap the water's surface. The water blurs the pale reflection at the touch, and the moon-shape sends its ripples out to meet my shoes' indentions in the mud. Beyond the edge of night sound several rustlings: they're gone as soon as I glance up to look for them, and all I see appears to be a muted echo of the campfire in the headlights of the truck. Fiery eyes waiting, watching us.

Farther off, away, coyotes cry.

Ky-oats, my father says. I think he must sense my worry. He pokes the fire with the stick and stares into the heat with a certain kind of softness weighted in his features, his eyes. Like he's waiting for nature to explain itself. *They're singin' to find each other.*

And I hear them, sometimes, when we're back at home. From my bedroom, when I'm trying to sleep, trying to block out that noise. Our house sits surrounded by cotton fields: some of them, my father's; others, farmed by neighbors. And in the middle of the night, there are no sounds except the ones we make. But the coyotes, their voices lift up quick and hit a sound not unlike pain. Not unlike screaming. Those nights, I pull the covers up to just below my eyes and stare at moonglow on my window. I wonder at how far away they are. How close. I wonder at their progress, and the trails they make on that marked land. What they hunt for. If they're successful. I wonder who it is they've lost, or who they sing to find. (If coyotes think like that.)

Even still, almost twenty years later, when I hear the howling of a neighbor's dog (I've since left coyote-song behind for city music), I feel the hair along my arms lift up. I feel a chill shift through me. It's a sound like muscle memory, and my body seeks out something like an answer. First there's fear, and then there's knowing. An understanding. (Remembering.) That everything sings out for a reason. To find something, maybe, what's been lost. Each other.

When I hear the howling-out of anything, my father's pond floods back: there, in the tent, my father's snoring keeps me up, and the singing of coyotes closes in. I shiver in my sleeping bag imagining *the end*: sharp teeth and our family's God in Heaven. I think of reaching for my father, but I find I'm too afraid to move. So, I listen close to their approach: their nearness to the water, to the tent. To us. I hear the shuffling of feet and the lapping of tongues. There's more than one, I think—

And now the singing's stopped.

The world outside the tent falls into silence, sudden, closing in, and I wait up to listen.

ON ROADSIDE CROSSES

I'm headed out West, on the beginning of that 300-mile stretch toward home, when the first cross I see looms up tall beside the road. I'm 26, and even still, it feels like it's a beckoning: the steeple of a church, what's pointed sharp at Heaven. It casts a shadow in the parking lot ahead of it and stretches thin, and on, until it hits US 380. I'm not quick enough to catch what's written on the sign out front—the denomination that meets there—because I turn back to the road, fast, and I slam, hard, on my brakes. I skid on smoke to a stop. Catch my breath. Just a mile out of Denton, Texas, I think, and I've already almost crashed my car into a truck's trailer. Still, I click a pen. Spread out an old fast-food receipt along the steering wheel. I slash the first tally mark. I'm aiming to make note of all the crosses that I pass.

†

At 8 or 9 or 10 (or maybe, probably, sooner), I go to sit cross-legged in a circle with my parents, on my parents' bed. They're both in their pajamas: my father, shirtless, wears plaid baggy pants with drawstrings hanging down; my mother wears thin gray sweatpants, a loose pink t-shirt, and she rubs lotion on her hands. I'm in my pajamas too: a Batman symbol spreads across my chest. I must've said I'm ready for this. That I need Jesus in my heart, and now, *right now*. I'd always been a Christian, I thought, but I'd since been told that thinking's not enough. That to be a Christian means to be *convicted*. To be baptized, and, before you get there, to ask for Christ's acceptance. (Or: the other way around.) This—the asking for the potential of renewal—it comes, I think, alongside my recent fear of death. In front of my father, there's his open Bible. Its words—holy, hard to grasp—are marked up in a mustard yellow. And there's another book beside it: a how-to book, and a creased page whose heading reads, "How to Ask Jesus into Your Heart." "Dear God," my father reads the script, and so I say, *Dear God*. "I come to You a sinner," *and I ask for Your forgiveness*. "I know that Jesus," *Your only Son*, "died for my sins." *I ask for Christ, my only Lord and Savior*, I say, and I repeat, *to come into my heart*. We all hold hands—my father's, rough from work; my mother's, soft from all her constant rubbing—and we pray.

†

I used to have this fear that my parents might suddenly, without any sense of warning, pass away. Then again, I guess it was never really that they'd *pass away* but *die*—and always in a car crash. This built up early patterns: in class, I'd have to blink, quick, five good times, or else that siren that I heard outside the window might be headed to recover the twisted body of my mother; at home, the doorknob to my bedroom required five short turns before the final one could open up to lead me in or out, or else my father might fall off his tractor, get crushed under giant wheel and plow. I'd tap my feet, I'd bob my head; I'd glance at something on TV and look away and back again, away, and back, again. Five times. Like to the towers burning. To black dots like flightless birds plunging down their sides. To everything, falling, in what felt, to me, like an endless months-long loop at my mother's nail appointments. My mother's nail lady, she'd click her mouth. *Did you know,* she'd say, *that if you pause it right* . . . And she'd nod her head toward the television. To all that black smoke rushing out before the great dust plume of the collapse . . . *you can see the face of Satan?* And my mother, she'd shake her head. She'd sit and wait for all the color on her nails to dry. On the nights my parents would go on dates— out of that farm country, way out of our small town, and into Lubbock: forty minutes away—they'd leave me with my grand- parents. I remember how heavy waiting felt. I remember believing that, inevitably, the phone would ring, and I would answer: some strange and solemn voice on the other end would tell me about the wreck on some dark road, and then I'd know that they'd never be coming back to get me. In this belief, there was the fear that every- thing would change. My grandparents watched a different news network before bed—Channel 5 to my parents' 11—and this felt lonely; my grandparents rocked in a silence broken only by the sometimes-squeak of my grandfather's chair, while, on nights at home, my father filled the room with news about his day—and the chance of this change, of my father's voice, missing, felt lonely too. I feared my family's end, so I accepted the forever of a promised afterlife: and accepted, and accepted, and accepted, and accepted.

†

If we have been planted together in the likeness of his death,
we shall be also in the likeness of his resurrection . . .
—ROMANS 6:5

†

The day I'm told I should remember is a cold one. I'm 8 or 9 or 10, and outside, there's snow on the ground. I remember that: snow sticking—mounding up, and holding to the wind. We're on the edge of Lubbock, Texas, in one of the city's many churches, where, in 2002 (or '03 or '04)—apart from three cars marking color in that expanse of white—the enormous lot sits empty. It's my family: father, mother, little sister; my grandparents; our pastor, a man my father's age that I'll call J, and his wife. I think I might be wearing swim shorts. And a t-shirt. Like I'm going to the pool in the dead of winter.

†

I think about the road ahead and the distance here to home and my almost-crash into the trailer on the very edge of leaving. I think about how my memory's not so different: how my past appears in sudden flashes, still, ahead of me. At points along the road. I pass a small town's water tower, fat and heavy in the sky. It bears a cross with thick black arms painted on its side. Faded. I etch another line on the receipt. I set it in the passenger seat, and I look back to the road. And I worry, sometimes, about how memory exaggerates. How it might create from nothing. I worry that what I believe I've lived, that what I've seen, isn't really how life happened. That it's just one version of the truth: in some ways, maybe, a false belief.

But then, it isn't *lying*, I think. It's the process of seeking out that truth in pieces. It must be why I'm doing this: marking all the roadside crosses. To note, in some small way, a distancing. On either side of my car, the flattened world comes at me fast. Or I speed through it.

†

The day I'm told I should remember, I really don't. Was it *really* a temporary baptistry? Something built-up, placed there for that morning? Surely not—surely, we used what was permanent, in the church. And still, I'm inclined to think, for whatever reason, that we used something like a metal drinking trough. Like those for animals. So, say that's the truth, and picture it like this: row after row after row of red-cushioned chairs like modern pews sit in a too-big auditorium with hanging stage lights (turned off) and overheads (turned on, and dim). My mother stands, and my father holds the camcorder—his eyes hang onto what's real, and so the post-image of the camera comes out shaky and unfocused. My grandparents sit in the front row, my little sister on a lap. Pastor J stands in water to his knees. He's tall, red-headed; his voice holds a playful twang that crescendos to conviction, over and over again. I stand in the water, and maybe it hits my waist. Pastor J holds me in his arms, and he dips me under the water, and I think I must know what to do because I've done it many times before.

†

As a kid, we used the troughs for pools. I'd swim, naked, where my father's cattle drank; where frogs lined up along the edges, and I'd catch them, dunk them in. I'd watch them kick and swim and keep a few for the terrarium I got one year for Christmas, with its swimming pool and tiki hut. Its frog's small paradise. At my cousins' house, we'd run inside their trough in circles so that our feet beat quiet rhythm onto the metal floor like far-off timpani. We'd push against the water, running fast and getting faster, and we'd let our bodies go: go floating limp along the current of the whirlpool that we'd made, go spinning down into its center.

†

I guess it's not absurd that I'd be baptized in a trough. The absurdity, I think, comes more-so in the fact that there'd be one in the building in the first place.

†

A website touting tips for more remote sorts of baptism cites the trough as among the most common unconventional baptistries. Others include inflatable hot tubs and standalone fiberglass constructions. Movie theater lobby fountains. There's the Portable Baptistry (starting at $2,499) and a smaller, more affordable option, the Portable Baptistry Jr. ($999). Throw in something reviewers call the Heavenly Heater for comfort, because, really, "nobody likes to get in cold water."

†

"Thousands Going Wild for Jesus!" one headline reads. "Unending Baptisms in Cow Troughs!" it continues.

†

Pastor J asks for my profession through his short red beard, and I guess I must profess. At 8 or 9 or 10, so whatever form that takes. "Do you believe that Jesus Christ is the Son of God?" *I do.* "That He died for your sins, to live again?" *I do.* "Do you accept Him—" *I*—"—as your Lord and Savior?"—*do.* And in the name of the Father, the Son, and the Holy Spirit, Pastor J cradles my back and presses firm against my chest to dunk me down into the water, to lift me up: and I am born again. My family in the front row claps, and the empty auditorium echoes with a sound that starts up, steadies, like some farmer's long-awaited rain's beginning.

†

The first (and only vivid) baptistry I remember looked bright and baby blue—not unlike the first bathtub I ever played in. The difference in the two was that which sprawled across as backdrop: where my first bathtub sat beneath a child's disarray—an alphabet, jumbled, plush, and colorful, pasted on a white tile wall to be arranged and disarranged, arranged again, in all my early bathtub splashing—behind the baptistry, in that age-old country Church of Christ, my grandmother had painted for the congregation a forest scene. With a river and tall mountains and pine trees. I suppose a scene like this can lend illusion: the belief that baptism is as natural a thing as nature itself. Now, that country church is gone, and in its place sits big bright yellow tubs of oil and tanks of gas fenced-off, for farmers and machines. But the landscape remains: flat and broken by new plows and old men, their sons.

†

*And the eunuch said, See, here is water; what doth hinder
me to be baptized? And Philip said, If thou believest with
all thine heart, thou mayest. . . . And they went down both
into the water, both Philip and the eunuch; and he baptized
him. And when they were come up out of the water, the
Spirit of the Lord caught away Philip, that the eunuch
saw him no more: and he went on his way rejoicing.*

—ACTS 8:36–39

†

My family doesn't lift our hands until we do. With palms turned
up and arms stretched out, like the ceiling might collapse. Like
it's our job for us to hold it. And when we lift our hands, we close
our eyes. Or I do. At 8 or 9 or 10. My little sister does. My mother
does, until she volunteers to play the tambourine up front for worship. And my father—maybe he holds on to tradition. Or else, he
has a hard time letting go, letting loose. Praising God so loud, so
publicly. At any rate, my father sings, but he keeps his body still.

†

We don't lift our hands until we change churches. I remember
standing outside my grandparents' house. We must've gone over
for a family dinner, or to tell them what we're doing. Or, likely,
both. The men—my father and his two brothers, their father—
grill up the burgers, and the women—my mother, my grandmother, and my aunts—sit around a table talking in the kitchen.

With empty plates, my father stands to tell the room we're leaving the Church of Christ—his family's foundation—for something new in town: hipper (though he can't say this), younger (I know it must've been on his mind). I think that I remember my grandmother holding tight against my father, crying hard against her son. Near-collapse. With head shakes, controlled. Her bird-like features—her harsh aquiline nose—drawn up as if in disgust. I imagine that she didn't, couldn't, look at my mother. (Though, I can't know that for sure.) But my closest cousin, slightly older than me and old enough to know how great the change, in this memory she holds on to me too. Squeezes me. Marks my Spider-Man t-shirt with her tears. She acts, I think—they all do—like my family might be going somewhere far away or dying.

†

Our new church, with its white rock facade and a smell like still-wet paint, sits tucked between old buildings on an often-empty side-street in our town. The children's room is cool. Cement floors, neon green walls. A smoke machine and blacklights and several flashing lasers. There's a foldout table up against one wall with three TVs sat one against the other all across. Behind the TVs, or ahead of them, or beside them, there's an Xbox and a PlayStation and a Nintendo 64. After church, most nights, I sit in front of these screens and aim and shoot at my friends, or we sit and aim and shoot at each other. One night, I hear a character on the screen tell another *Go to Hell*, and I run, and I tell my father. Who tells Pastor J. Who, probably, tells the children's minister: his wife, a short and smiley woman we call Miss K. I don't remember what all comes of this, just that we're told to mute all future sound.

†

These years, we tune our radios to songs of praise. In my grand-mother's car, in the backseat with my cousin, I tell them that *we have to change the music* unless we want to go to Hell. At school, on rainy days, I tell my teachers that I have to step out into the hallway, to sit alone against the wall, because I'm not allowed to watch the movie with the wizard boy and witchcraft. At home, and at the insistence of a friend from church, my mother makes me throw away what's in the box under my bed. *Demonic,* she says, of those trading cards, those brightly colored monsters. I walk them to the trashcan. I dump them in the trashcan's open maw. Later, my father takes the bag and burns it in the rusted cans behind the house, and I stand back to watch the fire eat holes around the plas-tic. I cry, and I might scream, and there's a gust that runs warm past my standing on the edge. The soft wind carries my noise, a brush against my father's loose denim work shirt, and it agitates the fire enough to spit its ash. I watch the gray bits hang the wind. I watch them as they float off, away, and land to bury in my father's field.

†

My best friend from church has kind eyes. A voice that rasps. He laughs often, and when he does, his kind eyes squint as if they're catching too much sun. D's family lives inside a mobile home right on the edge of town. This isn't strange, just different from what I'm used to. From his bedroom, you can hear the low vibrations of his mother's stepping in the kitchen; his older brother's picking at an electric guitar in the room across the hallway; his father's working on an engine in their home's front drive. There's a smell that hangs like pictures on the walls—unlike my house, my mother's several candles—like the fried foods of D's mother's cooking. One day, D's father tells the church about his gift. How he sees demons, or that he can. That, sometimes, they just appear. He says he's sitting home alone when it happens: that he looks up from his chair to see a figure in the kitchen. A dark shadow, hovering over the cream linoleum. With deep red eyes like orbs, floating where a face should be. He tells our congregation how he stands and plants his feet into the living room carpet, like he's bracing for a hit. How he starts to pray. To say, *In Jesus's name,* staring into that dual red, *I cast you out, in Jesus's name, I cast you out!* And the shadow— what D's dad had called the demon in his kitchen—snaps away. No sound, no impact. No evidence. As a kid, I think about this often. Every time I step into their kitchen, I stare at the floor; the sink; the cabinets, slightly raised above my gaze. Where I imagine eyes to be.

†

Sometimes Miss K orders pizza. Sometimes we get to come to church wearing pajamas. And these are special nights: middle-of-the-week nights, when the adults all file into the auditorium and close the doors and talk about who-knows-what for hours. One night, it's pizza *and* pajamas, and I wear big brown grizzly bear slippers. They're clawed, of course, and they're plush and hard to walk in. They contrast the rest of me: blue from top to bottom, in a cotton shirt and pants that reflect—if I remember right—some several swirling galaxies. I've been sick with something. (I'm unsure, now, what it was—a cold, maybe, or something just as minor, though I suspect I may have been unsure then too.) And still, in my memory, I fill my own plate up with pizza. I run around with other kids. And I run until my parents are, suddenly, there. Standing in the doorway of the children's room to get me. I protest that *the pizza's just arrived!* That *Miss K's just started the movie!* And I'm bummed until they tell me that the night's not over. That I'll be coming back, I just need to go with them first. I follow my parents out the door, into the hallway. Across the lobby. And through the closed double doors of the auditorium.

†

Imagine how this looks: a young boy dressed up like space and wearing big brown grizzly bear slippers—sick, apparently, with *something*—steps into the chapel. He runs the back of one hand across his nose and, maybe, I'm not sure (is he too old for this? at 8 or 9 or 10?), he holds his mother's hand with his other. His father walks close, ahead. They walk between rows of staring faces. Smiling faces. Oh-my-goodness-look-how-those-slippers-shift-his-whole-proportions faces. And the slippers *do* look far too big, because, well: that's the point. It's comedy, and it's comfort. And they look heavy too. In fact, the young boy thinks they feel like giant stones tied tight to his feet, with so many adults watching, and he has a hard time picking them up—one after the other after the other. But he does, and all the way down the aisle. To Pastor J standing there, up front.

†

Is there music? Singing? I can't imagine there'd be silence. And yet, that's how the moment sounds in my mind. There's the low hum

of the air conditioner. The rumble of the building, electricity running through it. Like a modernist soundtrack. And then, the rows
and rows of faces: staring back. Red chairs—always red chairs. Pastor J at that walk's end. He holds his left wrist with the grip of his
right hand. His Bible dangles just below his belt, and he smiles,
slightly, beneath his trimmed red beard.

†

A group of men stands up—three or four—and my father joins
them. Maybe my mother lets go of me here and sits. (I don't know.)
But just as I'm closing in on Pastor J, I look down at his feet, or,
near his feet, at the men and women on their backs. Their eyes
are closed. One man mumbles something under breath. He cries.
One woman trembles next to him like she's seizing—something
that my cousin does, too, sometimes, with bright white and sudden flashes on a TV screen—and this woman cries too. They roll
slightly on their backs like dying beetles, I think, on the sidewalk.
Like they're in pain, and the men that stand above those lying, *crying,* on the floor, they're smiling. Like Pastor J, whose eyes I meet.
Whose stare looks almost wild, and whose lips speak, *Jesus's name.*
His voice, I think, is sweet. Strangely, I think, like a kind of coming home. He reaches out to me with his palm stretched wide as
the group of men surround us. *In Jesus's holy name,* and he places
his hand against my forehead. *Heal this boy.* And he mumbles out
in tongues. *I ask for you to heal this*—he pushes, I fall back, and all
the men step up to catch me—*boy.* I close my eyes, and as I do, I
feel the rough hands of my father, gentle on my neck.

†

Imagine how this looks: a young sick boy dressed up like space and wearing big brown grizzly bear slippers lies on his back on the floor of a chapel. The big brown grizzly bear slippers aim their claws to the ceiling of the room. They loom over his small form. Women, mothers, whisper smiles. Men, fathers, can't help but laugh. He stays quiet. Keeps his eyes shut so that he only hears the sounds.

†

When Paul placed his hands on them, the Holy Spirit
came on them, and they spoke in tongues and prophesied.
—ACTS 19:6

†

I'd seen it many times before. That's how I knew how to fall. How to let men catch me, set me down, gently, on the floor. How to keep my eyes closed through the preaching and the prayer. How to not get up until I'm prompted to. To not speak into the mic until spoken to. To say *Yessir, Amen,* to Pastor J's *Do you feel it? The Holy Spirit runnin' through ya?* To hear my small voice echo around the room.

†

I never feel it. I want to feel it, so I try to feel it. I don't. And on and on and on and on and on again.

†

There's one time that I think I feel it. Or something close to it. I'm

12 years old and sitting in another chapel in Lubbock. This chapel's part of the church where I go to school. It's the middle of the day, and I'm alone in here. The room holds dark, or something close to it, because the teacher insists that the lack of light will help us pray. Her students spread about the building to close their eyes in corners or in pews or other isolated spaces. Where, still, with Jesus in my heart, I'm taught to seek Him in this Bible class. I use what I have learned, over years and years of watching. Of attempted reaching. Of being taught. I string together sounds like foreign objects on my tongue; I do this under breath, and I pick up speed, and I roll my *R*'s and land some letters hard against my palate. When, suddenly, there's a voice that speaks up in my head. When, suddenly, there's a stirring in my heart—or, in the space where I believe the Spirit to be—and the voice, the stirring, they force me to look. At nothing: at the dim outline of my feet planted firmly on the ground and the hands clasped tight together in my lap.

†

I can't remember the voice of God, but I remember His stirring. How the feeling left me just as quickly as it settled in.

†

If anyone does not have the Spirit of Christ,
they do not belong to Christ.
—ROMANS 8:9

†

I remember a boy in our church I'll call L. He's in high school. He's tall, skinny. Quiet. His voice, when he speaks, keeps at a higher pitch than the other boys his age. When he walks, his body follows in a jerk. His shoulders hunch. He holds himself together with arms wrapped tight around his stomach. And his face: at any time, it's either bored or angry. I don't see L much—not even at church—but when I do, it's rare nights at his family's house. (My father grew up with his.) When we're over for dinner, he lurks in his bedroom, the space between his bedroom and the bathroom, the bathroom. He's like a shadow in the hallway. On the drive back home, I learn the reason why he looks so different from his family. Why he doesn't share his father or his mother's face. He's *adopted,* my parents say. I learn this because he's just "*come-out*" to his family. I'm 8 or 9 or 10, and I try to understand but don't. I hear my parents wonder how L's father could've gotten it so wrong, how he ever raised a kid to be . . . and my parents pause, and they remember: that L's not his, not *really.* He is, but then he isn't.

†

Sometimes Miss K takes her children's ministry to the McDonald's down the street. We walk there, it's so close—and there are so few of us to watch. She orders ice cream cones for all of us. A large fry for the table. She takes one from its holder and dips it into chilled white. We laugh and scrunch the features of our faces. Call it gross. But she insists: says, *Try it.* So, we each grab a fry at the center of the table. We dip our fries into ice cream. I'm hesitant, but I bite down. It's salty, sweet. Good. *See,* she says, and goes back for another. *You just gotta trust me.* She presses vanilla on her tongue and smiles.

†

D's brother's room stays dark, and I'm not so sure we're both allowed to be here. He starts up his brother's Sega Dreamcast, and it's zombies. It's blood, guts, splattered on the screen. We shoot them, curtains blocking out the sun, the outside world, with controllers-like-guns. Sometimes, when we go outside and run around, we fake zombies out of nothing. We aim our hands at trees, and at the sky. We climb the half-pipe that his brother built one summer, aim at his family's sheep in the pen at its base. (D slides down the half-pipe as the sheep let out their calls; I climb down, slow, until both feet embrace the ground.) At the diner D's family owns—an old carhop, popular in town and bearing D's family's name—he takes me to the back: through the dining room, the arcade, and into the storage space behind an EMPLOYEES ONLY sign. The dining room walls are covered with scribbled names—the names of both our fathers, and their friends, and even those before them. But in the back, in the storage room, the walls remain bare. Nameless. The solid tan of unpainted wood. That is, until D uncaps a pen and writes his name—claims the space—and I write mine nearby, beside him.

†

The road back home, back to West Texas, I think, feels endless when you're on it. City landscapes melt away for white-bricked county courthouses and beaten-up Ford flatbeds and empty general storefronts. And then—mesquite mesquite mesquite, with angry branches filling out the landscape like closely scattered piles of skeletal remains. I stop in some small town like this, with a name that I'll forget every time I leave it. I pull up to the station. Park my car. Look down to the receipt that I have flattened in my lap. And I count them up: just over thirty crosses by the halfway point to home. I wonder why it is I'm really doing this, when I leave my car and go inside. Pass down aisles of wide-brimmed cowboy hats and sermons-on-CD and plastic dashboard crosses. (I note them, but I don't count them.) I step inside the bathroom where I stand, shoulders back, beside some white-bearded trucker at the urinal. He makes loud breathy sounds, like he's really trying here. Trying, maybe, to compete with the country music pumped in from the speaker right above us. It hisses with static. Against the hiss of our streams. And there's the temptation—felt, I think, because it's wrong, because curiosity has bad timing—to look down. To glance, just slightly to the other man. But I quickly find myself. And I see flashes of myself: with a broken, bloodied nose. Two eyes, swollen shut. A body, twisted, on the side of the road. I stare straight at the wall. I finish, wash my hands. I look up at the trucker looking back from where he stands, and our eyes meet in the mirror for a moment. Long enough to notice it, to feel as if I have to leave, and now. I rub my hands against my jeans as I walk out and to my car. I sit there. The car shakes alive, me in it. I pull away as the trucker walks outside and look to the rearview before the man can see me. I leave the station. I pause—turn, converge back on the road. I hit 50, 60, 65, 70, 75, I'm reaching, 80, and I coast. Not too far out from that drive-through town, there, at the base of a telephone pole—a roadside memorial, with a faded name and picture at its cross's center. Flowers, dead and scattered in the ditch. I reach for the receipt in the passenger seat, the pen in the cupholder. I etch another line.

†

These days, still, driving home from anywhere, I'll pick up some odd memory-scent of an old church's children's room, with its Jesus and its Mary and its Joseph all lined-up in felt against the wall. I'll sense the metallic weight of Christ's blood on my tongue, a taste like Welch's grape juice. I'll hear, or think I hear, the shuffling of women through their purses for mints and coins for offering. And why? I'll tell you—and here we get the Truth—that I've tried for almost ten years now to put some distance between myself and God. Between myself and Christianity. Between myself and, sometimes, *family.* But then, what happens when the self is tied-up in what it's tried so hard to move away from? Sometimes, I feel as if I'm running, attached to something, weighted, by a rope. That though I've stretched the greater length—and though I know that length's behind me—I'm forever tied to it, *bound* to it. And there's the knowledge, clear to me in this feeling, that even if I were to break away completely—from whatever holds me at the other end, some worn identity—the rope will go on hanging round my neck. Wherever I go: the excess of my memory, a noose long tightened to myself.

†

One day—and still, I'm 8 or 9 or 10—Miss K stands in the children's room, up front. Ahead of all of us. She's talking about God and how He speaks to us. How we might speak back to Him. *In tongues,* she says. *Who's heard of tongues?* I have, and so I raise my hand with all my friends around me. Like roll call. My little sister—she's a row or two ahead—she raises her hand too. *Good,* and

Miss K smiles. *Now,* she says in a sing-song sort of way, *Who here knows how to* speak *in tongues?* I raise my hand with all my friends around me. But I don't know how to speak in tongues. I've never spoken in tongues.

†

I just don't want to be the outcast.

†

My little sister sits still. Her glasses appear thick where they frame her eyes and reflect, at an angle, the bright light of the room. Her hair looks big and brown and bushy. She folds her small hands together in her lap. She does not know how to speak in tongues. She does not know, yet, how to lie.

†

My little sister's the outcast. The only one who says that she can't do what Miss K's asking. And Miss K puts her hands together. Smiles, nods her head. Like she's made a new discovery. *Thank you,* she says, to my little sister, *for your honesty.* Miss K puts a movie on and walks over to my little sister, reaches out. My little sister takes her hand and stands. They walk over to the doorway, what leads out into the lobby of the church, and Miss K switches off the lights. My friends, my little sister's friends, all stand up and get comfy. Bean bags and pillows. Blankets for further comfort. I stand to find a spot when I hear my name across the room. I look behind me, to the open door: to Miss K and my little sister standing, silhouetted, in the lobby's pale-yellow light. *Come on,* Miss K says. *Come hold your sister's hand.* The two of them don't move until I do.

†

The lobby's bright and white with random chairs and tables spread with books and pens and crosses. There's a bookstore near the entrance with the books whose titles promise *health* and *prosperity* and *happiness.* With brown leather Bibles and orange Tic Tacs and white Mentos, all for sale. Miss K leads us across the room past racks of items and the huge cash register on a countertop. She opens the door on the opposite end of where we came from, that children's room. To Pastor J's office. And before we step through, I hear the muffled sounds of Pastor J's preaching on the other side of the double doors nearby. And the lifting-up of voices, *Amens.* My parents: indistinct among them.

†

Inside the room that's like a cave, there's a droning through the walls. The service, on the other side, can still be heard. The words sound without form, but the voice: it holds on to the air in here and hums. Miss K sits behind Pastor J's desk, and my little sister and I sit in the two chairs across from her. They're big to our small, and plush, and almost comfortable. Behind Miss K, on the wall, there's a painting like a rainbow: faded, jagged lines of color bleed across the canvas. The whole thing frames her head. Her smile. And I can't help but feel like I'm in trouble. Like we've both been caught for doing something wrong—my little sister by admission, and myself by no fault here but relation.

†

Today, sometimes, I search for answers. At the bottom of a YouTube video in which a pastor discusses the role of tongues in the Bible—a controversial topic—a woman comments: "When I want to pray for things I don't know how to pray for, like world problems, our government and what's going on in our country, etc., God knows how we should pray when I don't. So, praying in tongues gives me that ability through my spirit, by the Holy Spirit." She continues: "I heard of one man that was praying in tongues at a church meeting and a Native American man said to him, 'I didn't know you could speak our language.' The man didn't know how to speak his native language, he was just speaking in tongues and it came out as that language. So, after hearing this the Native American man received Jesus." She concludes: "All Christians should receive the Baptism of the Holy Spirit and speak in tongues."

†

On the same video, another comment: "Speaking in Tongues is nothing but gibberish nonsense." Another: "Speaking in tongues is just babbling."

†

And another, a believer: "I'm going to evangelize my family using these videos."

†

Miss K looks my little sister in the eyes and tells her that she'll learn to speak like angels. Says it's a gift that she can give. One that my little sister can use to praise God, *hallelujah, forever and ever—Amen.* Miss K looks me in the eyes and asks for my help. My guidance. (I'm 8 or 9 or 10.) She gestures to my little sister in the other chair. *Your sister.* Miss K smiles. Teeth white like vanilla. Like salt. *Why don't you show her how it's done?*

†

In a different YouTube video titled "Eden, 6 years old, interpreting a word of tongues" [*sic*], a 6-year-old girl named Eden does just that. Or claims to. A tall and skinny balding man with glasses and a microphone stands in front of a wooden cross, a deep blue wall. He addresses his congregation: "We have a testimony from Eden this morning," and he smiles, and there are cheers and claps and laughs from all those out of frame. His Australian accent flows gently out of him. Smooth. Like healing water. "She told me last night, and I was, just"—he sucks in air and pulls his hands up to his chest like he can't contain what's coming—"*blown away.*" The girl we're told is Eden stands to the tall man's waist. She smiles hard and twists her body back and forth to twirl the black dress that falls to just below her knees. On the front of that black dress is a big pink prize ribbon—for what, we can only imagine. Having cracked the Code of God? Having earned her place, at 6 years old, in Heaven? Maybe; maybe. After the tall man directs her—where to stand, where to look, where to speak into the microphone—he passes on the mic and steps back. Eden rattles off, immediately: "I heard Liz speak in tongues, and she was saying, 'Yes, God, yes.'" She smiles, proud, before she steps away. Hands back the microphone. There are happy rumblings from the congregation. Some clapping. One woman's louder with her praise than the rest. The tall man laughs. Says Eden tells it straight. Then he, the adult on stage, gives us, the audience, some context: that in the children's ministry, they'd written godly gifts on scrolls of paper. That these gifts had gone into a bowl, and, "apparently," all the kids had fished one out. That Eden drew *the interpretation of tongues*. And the congregation can't contain its excitement. They can't believe it, this miracle. They *Wow* and they clap. One man laughs: not at the absurdity of the event but because Eden—standing to the side— makes a face that he must think is cute.

†

"So, it's simple," the tall and skinny balding man says. (Eden's message, he means.) "But—it's actually quite meaningful."

†

Suddenly, a younger girl runs up on stage and wraps her arms around Eden. Is she a sister? we wonder. A friend from class? In any case, this act is met with laughter as she turns to smile at the crowd. And when she pries herself away, she's out of frame. "Maeve," the tall man smiles, points at the younger girl that, now, we cannot see. "Which gift did *you* pick?" From the bowl, he means. From the children's ministry. The tiny voice sounds unsure. Sounds more like a question. "The—" There's hesitation. "—the tongues one?" At once, the distant voice of some older woman, far out of frame, calls out, quick: "*No! Healing!*" And the tall man laughs. And the congregation laughs. And the children—you can tell from their faces—do not understand that the younger girl has lied. That, maybe, both of them have.

†

I cannot lie alone. Not without my friends around—and certainly not where God's concerned. I stare at the face of Miss K, who waits for me to speak. To demonstrate. My little sister looks at me, too, and I notice how her smile turns up slightly at the corners of her mouth. There's an excited sort of energy in her gaze. Her whole demeanor. Like she's anxious for allowance. Like she's standing at a door that only I can open, and she's waiting for me to let her in.

†

One night, at home, it's just my father and me. He cooks us dinner (I'm at least 5 in this memory, though probably—surely—older than that), and we wait for 8 o'clock. For the movie that's premiering on TV: *The Mummy*. We'd seen the trailers for weeks. Had marked out the time to watch it as a kind of bonding. Father-son. My mother acts cautious before she goes, with my baby sister, wherever she ends up going. She wonders about the content of the movie. But my father assures her: it's all cut for time. For the content that gives it its PG-13 rating. And besides, he says: we can always turn it off.

†

One night, Pastor J and Miss K invite my family over for dinner. I'm not sure why, what for, though I don't expect there was ever any reason beyond the fact that it's the job of this man and his wife to foster a congregation. I don't remember anything from the night other than this: after dinner, when my parents move to the living room to talk, I'm asked if I'd like to watch TV. I'm not sure where my little sister is in this memory—I'm just certain that Pastor J walks me back to his and Miss K's bedroom where I crawl up on their bed. Lie amongst the throw-pillows. I remember thinking, even then, on the strangeness of this. The intimacy. How lying on their covers in their bedroom in their house—it all felt wrong. But there's a large screen at the foot of their bed, and Pastor J turns it on with the click of a remote. He scrolls through the listings, and there it is: *The Mummy.* I'm not so sure he knows exactly what this is, but I ask for him to pick it, and he clicks the movie. Leaves the room. Closes the door.

†

When Miss K asks for me to demonstrate for my little sister, I back down, and I confess: I'm not sure how to speak in tongues. I was afraid. Nervous. And so, I said I could when, in fact, I couldn't. I didn't want to be alone in this. I don't remember how Miss K looks at me then. I don't know if she's disappointed that I've lied in front of her and all my friends, my little sister, and to God. But I imagine that she might praise Him, however silently, for another student. A disciple. I imagine that she takes our hands and prays for us. Over us. That she's convicted she's imparting something on us we could never find ourselves. I do remember that she demonstrates. That the words that fall out from her mouth sound almost funny to my ears. Like a video played backwards. And then she asks us what we've heard. If we've understood it. If we'd be willing, now, to try.

†

Here's another confession: I learn to "speak" in tongues thanks, in part, to *The Mummy*. Sure, Miss K helps me. And I hear it, see it, all the time. But in the moments that I try—really *try*—to force out tongues, *The Mummy* is the model. It's when a character, translating from the Egyptian *Book of the Dead,* reads out slowly, like a chanting, with conviction. (And in turn, for better or for worse, it's this conviction that raises the dead.) So in the moments that I try—and I do, I really *try*—I close my eyes and think of Rachel Weisz and sheer black sleeves and hair that falls in loose curls over shoulders. I think of how she moves a perfect finger slow across thick metallic pages, how that finger glides beneath the several lines of packed-together hieroglyphics whose hidden meanings fill her mouth and tumble out harsh and, still, precise. How she picks up speed before her tongue hangs onto a single word: *yatuwe, yatuwe, yatuwe.* What raises the dead. I make it, then, my prayer, my demonstration: *yatuwe, yatuwe, yatuwe.* (Inhabit, inhabit, inhabit.)

†

And here's another confession: I'm 12 years old and visiting my grandparents' church. I don't remember why I'm there. Maybe just to make them happy. Or maybe it's near Christmas. Easter. In any case, I'm staring at the baptistry my grandmother painted all those years ago: the congregation had moved it here, to the new building they'd built in town, after that old country church fell apart. Since that time and my family's leaving, the congregation's fallen too: the sign on the wall beside the baptistry reads 52 in last week's attendance, and when I look around, all I see are familiar faces grown gray. And still, there are absences. Whole gaps between pews. I'm studying the sign when, suddenly, something moves through me. A kind of voice, in my head. My mind. A stirring, hard to resist, in the pit of my stomach. And near to my heart, where the Spirit might be. I silently excuse myself as the pastor drones on at the front. I can't remember what he's saying, but I'm sure it's not too far from *health* and *prosperity* and *happiness*. I walk to the back of the chapel and keep on walking, almost in a sort of rush now, down a hallway and to the bathrooms at the end. Once inside, I hurry to a stall. I step inside. Lock the door behind me. I stand, for a moment, looking down at the toilet's open mouth. The droning sound of my grandparents' pastor penetrates the walls. And I masturbate. It doesn't take long until I'm finished, and I flush the finish down and watch it disappear. I readjust myself. I stand in silence in the stall, waiting, I think, for something to happen. A bolt of lightning through the ceiling. The twisted fingers of the Beast to rise up, pull me through the tile. When nothing seems to happen, I leave. It's as I'm stepping back into the chapel that I feel something like a burning on my body: it's the eyes of that aging congregation, watching me walk back to find my place; it's God as the color blue, peeking through the pine trees of that painted baptistry.

†

Do you not know that your bodies are temples of
the Holy Spirit, who is in you, whom you have
received from God? You are not your own.
—1 CORINTHIANS 6:19

†

One day, in music class, at 8 or 9 or 10, we children lumber onto
metal stands lined with thin gray carpet. There's a stain near the
floor that we all try to avoid: a black blot marked, at one point,
early in the year, by some kid's throwing-up. So, we climb, because
when you're lucky, you're all the way up top. I'm lucky, and D's
almost-so: he sits one step below me, at my feet. When the bell
rings, the teacher turns off all the lights and switches on the projector. She clicks a button on the stereo—a small red dot fades
up in the dark—and skips through tracks until she lands on one:
"Jupiter, the Bringer of Jollity," a woman's voice, near-robotic, says.
"By Holst." Strings climb, brass blares; the timpani strikes. Hymns
had, I realize now, taught me how to appreciate music—as an ele-
ment of praise, sure (though the Church of Christ only ever per-
mitted praise-by-voice), but also as something just to be enjoyed.
Respected. Seated at the projector, capped marker in-hand, our
teacher follows the imagery of space: she points to planets, stars,
and comets that each represent a moment of the music's time.
She's far enough away from us, so focused on the music, that she
can't see D's quiet turning in his place to tell me something; that
she can't see my leaning forward to whisper something into D's
ear; that she can't see how, in perfect time, and to the swell of leit-
motif, the both of us meet perfect in the middle. My first kiss: an
accident. And it's quick—quick enough so no one in the dark has
seen it. But I remember looking with surprise at D looking back.
And smiling. Like the thing we'd meant to say had been a joke,
and it'd been really funny. I remember, too, how the memory of
that moment stretched to more than seconds in my mind. I think
the truth is that we both forgot to say the things we'd meant to say,

because he turned his back to me, and I looked back to the projector, to our teacher tapping time like it just might get away from us.

†

I remember a boy in our church I'll call Z. His flamboyance. Limp wrists and spiked-up frosted tips. The way his legs cross when sitting and his Hollister cologne. He's loud. Polite. He's the only boy in our small town in cheerleading. And he sounds, I think, like a girl. One day, what must've been a Friday night in fall, my family gets ready to leave our house for a high school football game. I'm 8 or 9 or 10. (Z, then, like that other boy L, is in high school.) I stand holding my sister's pom-poms in the kitchen. I lift a leg and kick, and my shoes squeak wild on the white linoleum. I jump and shake my body. Dance in rhythm to the music that I sing—and cheer what our cheerleaders cheer. A fight song. Until my father rounds the corner from the living room. Until he shakes his head and curls his nose, says, *Stop that,* stern, and I still. *We don't do that,* he says. My father's tone's the one reserved for trouble, and I know he thinks of Z here, because I do. *Boys don't act that way.* Boys, he says. *Real* boys, he means. Back at church, I notice how my father presses his hands deep into his pockets around Z. How my mother smiles back but drops it when we leave. In the car ride home, they tell me that I need to stay away from him. I don't know why—but I think (I must) that it has something to do with cheerleading.

†

At 12, it starts with one word: "naked," in the search bar of the laptop I get for Christmas. When my family goes to sleep, and I start an early life habit of staying up well past midnight. I add "women" to the search. Move onto, simply, "porn." "Masturbation." "Masturbation techniques." "Mutual masturbation." "Jerking off." "Circle jerk." "Handjob." "Blowjob." Then, inspired—curious: "men kissing." "Penis." "Naked men." My hand stalls then clicks through Google Images. I type, "gay." "Gay sex." "Gay porn." I watch. I stare. I don't know if I like it, but I think I do. I think I like it more than all the other stuff, at least, and I start picturing my classmates. My friends, in gym. Start noticing the hair that marks their bodies. Their underarms. What's started, now, to peek out, dark and wiry over waistbands. I gaze down at the floor when I change. I cover myself, to be sure. And when my eyes drift over, I make it quick. I steal a glance for later. For home: when, in the front room of my family's house—where I'm meant to keep my laptop overnight—I "masturbate" to "men making out" and "having sex." I do this for hours, I "edge" until I "cum." Into my hand, or onto my body, where I wipe it up. Clear the history. Close the laptop and sit in the dark, in the house's quiet. The wind against the windows. It's not wrong, I think, because it's only curiosity. There's nothing wrong about that. Nothing *sure* about that. And I go to sleep. Until, one night, I'm woken up in bed. It's my father in the doorframe, and there's the glow of some low light behind him. Etching out his form, like a shadow detached from its body. He says my name, and his voice is a tremor at 3AM. Like he, too, has just been woken up. He tells me that I need to get out of bed. To go with him. Now. He's stern, unusual. And he leads me through our house, where the only light—what was my father's doorway backlight—shines out from underneath the upper kitchen cabinets; it reflects dull inside the hearts of several crosses hung up in the living room: my mother's life's collection. And the A/C kicks on, and its sound is like a monstrous rumble in the walls. My father leads me through the doorway of the front room, where, in the chair I'd been sitting in just moments ago, my mother's face is lit up from my laptop's bright white screen. And my mother's crying: her brow is furrowed, furious, her eyes a deep, deep red. She sniffs. She shakes her head. My heart sinks. The hair along my arms lifts like the undead come to life. How, I think, how did they know? And, Why now? And, Why here? I sit beside my father on the couch that runs adjacent to the chair. My mother can't talk. She tries, but her words come out chopped. In fragments. She tries, but she stops herself from trying. I think she's horrified, at whatever it is she's seen. And *I'm* horrified at whatever it is she's seeing. And my father speaks for her. *Imagine,* he says, *if this were your sister.* And there's a confused sort of turning in my heart. (Where I still believe the Spirit might be. Where I think I've felt it, for a moment.) And there's remembrance: tonight—by some miracle— I've stuck to "women" in my searching. The months before, then, are history wiped clean. *They have brothers,* my father says, *like you. And fathers and mothers.* I can't read my father's face. His tone of voice. *Imagine if this was your daughter.* Almost monotoned. Still waking up. And my mother just keeps shaking her head. *It's wrong,* she manages to say. *Don't you know?* and she catches her breath. Collects the air that's frozen still, around us. I think that I could choke on the rest of what she leaves us. *Don't you know it's wrong?* And my cheeks are warm, hot. I'm sweating in my t-shirt. I'm looking not at either of the faces of my parents but to the carpet in the dark. Its white plush tints gray in the light that spreads out from the laptop's screen. That shines against my mother's wet and puffy cheeks. That hits the tan-toned wall behind her to dirty it gray too.

†

It is shameful even to mention what
the disobedient do in secret.
—Ephesians 5:12

†

One day, during recess, we children gather on the track. Some kids
walk between the rubber rows while others spread out on the field
at the track's center. D stands underneath the metal bleachers with
a friend. They wave me over. I glance around, make sure the three
of us stay outside the gaze of all our teachers. And I run. I get
closer, and they're laughing. D looks nervous, but his friend—a
city kid before our town, with the dark hint of hair on his upper
lip even now, at 8 or 9 or 10—he just keeps laughing. *A condom,* he
says. Points to the ground. At the thing like a deflated balloon half-
buried in the dirt. I'd never heard the word before. And from the
look that he was giving it, D hadn't either. So we cock our heads.
We laugh with the kid who knows. At this off-white creature—
what reminds me, then, of shed snakeskin—filled at its end with
something like a liquid. And the whistle blows, and we're running
back. *Condom,* I think. (But I soon forget the word.) The next day
we go back, it's gone. And the next—back on the playground, not
the track—we play "*Titanic*" on the big slide. All our parents have
it now, on VHS, and so we've seen it some before: the ship tilting
to its sinking pose, people tumbling down its decks. This game has
us climbing up and up the metal slide; we thumb the surface pock-
marks as we go; we reach the top, and we pull ourselves up, extend
a hand down to fellow passengers. *Come on!* I say to D, still climb-

ing. *Take my hand!* and he reaches out. And his hands: each finger's wrapped, today, in a colorful Band-Aid. When D takes my hand, I grip—and I ask him what they're for. All those Band-Aids. *Warts,* he says, and I let him go. I rub my hand until it's hot against my jeans and watch D slide down to the bottom. Into the icy waters: into the sandpit, where he stands up. Brushes off the layer of the dirt his clothes caught going down. And my best friend looks at me. And he looks to his hands. And I can't say why I did it.

†

Sometimes, then, I try to picture how it happened: when D, home alone (or alone, inside) let a tissue wave over a candle's flame. When he held it there, and he lowered it, curious, until it caught, too quick to stop it. I try to picture what it's like: to have fire race along one's body with a helpless speed. To watch it eat the skin of one's own hand. (A taste, I thought then and think still, of Hell.) I imagine how he screamed, and how that scream filled up the spaces of his house. His father may have been outside, working on a car—may have heard his screaming through the walls. Or else, D stumbled to the kitchen, to the place where his father's demon stood, to scream into the phone. To his mother, working at the carhop. Maybe he ran out the front door and to his grandma's house nearby. A short run—and I picture how he held his hand: ahead of him, in a claw, bright pink, raw; or maybe, clutched so near his heart. Like some fleshy spider dead on its back, curled into itself. In any case, D doesn't show for school one day, or church. Which is when we hear about it. And after school, my mother takes me to the Dollar Store in town. She buys a toy gun, and we say that it's from me: a sort of space thing, green, with a weighted orange trigger. And she buys candy, what I think he'll like. (What I know I like.) My mother takes me to D's house and waits inside the car. I'm nervous, but I want to go myself. His mother answers the door. And D stands behind her, his hand wrapped up in layers of egg-white cloth like a mummy's. Of course, I don't tell him that I want him to take it off—the wrapping. I'm not sure, then, that's even what I want. It's not until later, when I'm home and can't stop thinking of his skin. What it might look like, beneath the new protection, now that it's all gone. If he'll still wear his Band-Aids. If his warts were burned clean off.

†

> *Land that drinks in the rain often falling on it and*
> *that produces a crop useful to those for whom it is*
> *farmed receives the blessing of God. But land that*
> *produces thorns and thistles is worthless and is in*
> *danger of being cursed. In the end it will be burned.*
> —HEBREWS 6:7–8

†

I've long since moved away from myself; I've left a part of me behind. It's not that I want any of the time back—no, just that there are reminders, everywhere I go, of a life I lived. A memory of *before—memories* of before. And though I wish I could, I can't explain why some stand out like yesterday when the details of so many others have left me. So much of childhood's a haze, but scattered fragments remain.

†

When I pull into town—Post, Texas—I stop counting crosses. When I stop at a red light, I eye the marks on the receipt: 64. From there to here. And here, there are too many to count. They line the windows of the shops on Main Street. They stand tall, up from the ground outside the post office. The bail bonds building. The county courthouse. There's a cross on the marquee of the community theater. There's a cross on the outdoor menu—faded, now—of the carhop my old friend's family still owns. And there's a cross at the very center of the sign welcoming those of us returning home. My family—Mom, Dad, my little sister, and I—doesn't live here anymore, so I stay with the family that does. My grandparents' house, once far out in the country, sits on the edge of town. This is where I go. Past the Baptist church, the Methodist. The church where Pastor J and Miss K still speak to future generations. And my grandparents' Church of Christ. Where, nearby, every other house inside the neighborhood boasts crosses in front yards. Front porches. On flags flown high on poles. And on my grandparents' street, the backsides of enormous trucks bear cross decals. Or Scripture spread engraved along the glass. Or both. When I park my car, when I finally turn it off, I feel my heartbeat, furious inside me. My breathing's stalled. I rub each palm's sweat against the denim of my jeans, and I rub them, and I rub them, I rub them, and I rub them. (Old habits, here.) I pull the visor down and stare at my reflection. I hesitate—before I remove a piercing hooped in one ear, and then the other. I hold them in my hands, the skin of both palms so red from all that rubbing. Pieces of a self. I drop the piercings in the cupholder to rattle where they fall, and the harsh wind rattles the windows, and it pushes against the standstill car. The tree outside, it shakes, and the movement sounds like a storm starting up. I half-expect the window to pulse with spots of rainfall, and then

I remember where I am. I close my eyes. Feel my body rise with
breath. Feel it fall with a weight that settles me into the driver's
seat. I'm not myself in this old town, I realize—or else, I've grown
beyond the self that called this place a home. Out my window, I see
movement: the front door, opening, and my grandmother standing in it. She lifts a hand and waves it. Smiles. She steps down onto
the sidewalk, and she wanders to my car. Her body's lean, more
like a bird's than ever, I think. Fragile. Anxious. She stares at every
future footstep, and when she stops, it's at the edge of driveway.
She picks at the skin of her thumb. She leans down to her garden, pulls a weed. She waits, I know, for me to step out onto the
street—and when I do, I feel the old home hit me; I feel the old
self settle in my skin: how it stings in dust caught in this place's
breeze; how it smells like oil and like cattle; how its eternal sound
is nothing. I meet my grandmother at the edge of sidewalk, and
she wraps her arms around me. She squeezes, and she presses firm
against my back with what strength she has. It's always then: I feel a
stirring near my heart where I once believed the Spirit to be—near
the place this family stood where I last left them.

GENERATIONS
(LIKE SURRENDER)

We're several miles from town, Post, Texas, where there's nothing much but cotton and the sky, and all around us it's the bare-slate land I'd once called home. I'm visiting from what feels far away—the Metroplex. I've ridden out with my father, and his, to load a couple of cattle into a trailer.

(And it takes no time to realize that I feel like less a man out here.)

I don't belong, I think. Not here, not anymore, at least. Anyway, I sure don't look the part: black jeans hug skinny to my legs, undirtied and near brand-new; my white Converse, the most worn part of me, appear stain-spotted gray along their sides; and my blue t-shirt, a hug against my belly, is just a shade or two darker than the bright sky that holds solid above us. It's the one constant, I think, the thing about this place that hasn't changed, that won't ever: that sky.

(And the country—here—*now*, I think, it makes me feel so small.)

I'm 26, and like a child, I'm stepping back to watch the work.

My father's found an old plow part. It's sizable, near rusted. Half-buried in the dirt. It's settled near the base of the leaning yellow house where we've stopped to get the trailer. Where several generations of my father's family learned to work, and hard. There's a picture of them here, what's tucked, yellow-faded, into one of my grandmother's many picture albums. It's the first generation lined and coupled up together, standing by the porch. My grandmother has made it her aim to document her family and her husband's family's history—*our* history—and she taps the corner when she pulls the photo out and shows me: *1925,* it says in chicken scratch, above the sepia earth. The men wear suits with vests or else something close: a dark pant with a dress shirt and a tie, and *they look,* I think, *like men.* Two women of the three wear white dresses where the matriarch wears black, and every dress meets skin or dark hose at just below mid-calf. All eight of those standing in the photo arch their shoulders forward as if some great weight has settled at the very moment they've been captured. Their row of faces stare toward the camera's lens, and the biggest smile is hardly one at all; their eyes must face the sun as they squint, tight, and their mouths appear as solid lines to match them. Even the youngest of this group—or the one who I imagine must be: the girl on the left of the porch's steps who can't be much older than 16, maybe 17—her body appears to struggle against itself, as if she's working to hold herself up from something unseen—some force that's pulling down and tying her to the earth. The man who stands up highest, on the first step of the porch beside his wife, he has my father's hands, and his father's hands. It's a small fist curled at the edge of a dress shirt's cuff—a tint darker than his face—cracked and lined with dirt.

Now, all these years later, my father's father—the man that I, my sister, my cousins and our parents all call *Grandaddy*—nearing 80—he helps my father raise the piece of plow. The movement shakes off dust, or well enough, so that it powders down and back into its place like snow. I step forward from my lean against my father's truck—what's bright, bright red, and, still, what's somewhat new to me—longing to do something, *anything*, with my hands. But Grandaddy waves me off with a nod of his head. And my father waves me off with a nod of his head. And the motion makes me wonder how they see me. If they think I might get hurt.

(They're gentle signs, I think. But there they are.)

I watch them as they carry that ancient weight. As they step quick, beside each other, shuffle over earth, to set it in the truck's bed. The truck bows to the burden, and they clap their hands, dull, together. Grandaddy leans down to beat the dust from off his boots with wadded-up work gloves.

It's a Sunday afternoon and far enough from morning to feel some early autumn heat. The air, today, is still; the wind, I think, is resting with the country. My father's still got on his church clothes, the red and white striped button-up tucked into dark blue jeans. And his jeans, like two great snakes, swallow over the tops of light-tanned boots, and the long sleeves of his shirt are cuffed, starched, and extended down to both his wrists. Grandaddy's got on the same tan shirt he's always worn, with both sleeves rolled back to rest bunched up above his elbows. He's got the long white packet of his chewing tobacco curled up in his front pocket so that it bulges slightly, unforgotten at his chest. The difference now, I think, between himself and his son, between the past and the present, is in how this shirt hangs loose off his body. As if, for years, it's slowly worked its way—has finally won—at eating him alive.

I feel I'm very far away from them. The men of the family. The action of the plow. I look down, to my feet: to the crisscrossed pattern in the sand where our tire tracks have been. To a lizard there, dead. I can't know, really, if we'd killed it, or if it'd been there, dried-up, longer than today. But its guts have bubbled out from all that cracked gray skin in a neon yellow bulb like poison. From where I stand, my shadow casts a weight that tints its look. And the lizard looks like it'd been smiling, just before or long before the crush: its mouth hangs open, eager, and its eyes, too, half-so.

Small evidence, I think, of a world disturbed.

Grandaddy laughs. I hear his pat on my father's back. A soft slap, a whisper on fabric. "Sure good," he says, "to have somethin' to haul your junk in." He's talking, I think, about my father's truck. The plow. And his voice sounds like the world out here: deep and flat, with a hard sort of edge. His thick drawl drives ahead in a bass-level monotone that lifts at points to drop again in unexpected bursts—enough so that if you don't listen closely, you just might miss the turns.

"Do what?" my father asks, and I look up from the lizard's corpse. My father's smiling, but he hasn't really heard his dad.

"I said," Grandaddy starts again, and he repeats himself.

My father stands just above his dad. Just enough so that his eyes gaze down to talk. His gut's a greater bulge against his dress shirt where Grandaddy is a body shrinking. His arms aren't what they used to be: somewhere along the way, they've dropped the strength they used to carry—what was my father's strength, his son's— and his skin holds several scattered bruises that have appeared as extra color, marking work and age. Like my father's, his skin holds the heat of each day's sun, near-tinted red. (His family's claimed *Comanche blood,* but there's no hard truth to that.) Their hair's the same light shade of brown, as if they've learned, over both their lifetimes, to adapt to the earth that's always been familiar. A part of them. It's thin and almost free of gray, which is, already, different from my own: a border on black, thick, and curly, with hints of silver peeking through.

I look nothing like them. A different generation of man, I think, or a different son entirely.

MY FATHER'S childhood, he tells me, was constant work. Always dirtied hands and farmer's tans and cuts and scrapes and bruises. He'd wake up with the sun and head out to the fields with his father and his older brothers to pull the endless weeds and work until the mealtimes. Start again the next day. Grandaddy, he tells me, his father—the constant work is all he ever knew. And all his father ever knew. And all his father ever knew. And on and on, and back to the beginning.

At the end of my growing up, my father tells me that he always sought to raise a different kind of son; different, he means, not from *me* but from *himself*—and from that great line of work-weary sons that came before him.

Of course, in growing up, he still takes me fishing on his ponds. He takes me hunting for crawdads in the shallow streams around a family friend's property. He takes me hiking up the edges of the caprock. Those days, we carve our names in fallen trees and slip new pennies under rocks—a ritual my father started on our hikes, to mark the year—and we tell ourselves that we'll return one day to see, to claim them. (But the tree's been cleared from where it fell, and the pennies rest beneath their rocks, now—if they do— on a stranger's land.) And I sit with him while he works. He bangs against machinery, those great extensions of himself, and dots himself with oil. I hunt for cool rocks and arrowheads; I draw pictures in the dust with thin and broken metal plow parts; I catch fat horny toads that spit blood at me through dark beady eyes when I grip their waists and pet them on smooth spotted bellies. We drive out to his fields at harvesttime, when all the cotton plants are stripped to clean or else hold thin remains of what they grew like captured wisps of cloud, and my father lifts me up to climb, to run along the tops of the tall rectangular bales of cotton that he formed with those machines. On these, I feel my body start to sink, and the feeling holds a sharpness in it: the cottonseed that presses into my bare hands and sometimes feet. I sit inside my father's machines, small enough for the corner, behind his armrest, his shoulder, and I read to him above the buzzing tractor noise from chapter books. Those stories about kids and passing time and magic treehouses. Until he lifts a hand and says, *Hold on,* says, *Hold on, Bubba,* and he stops to get out. To climb down. To check whatever requires his stopping. When he climbs back in and settles, the machine moves with a jolt, and he pats me. Waves me on. I read until the sun goes down. Until I put my head against the window, and I try to sleep against the movement of a lonely world that shakes me head to toe. Until my mother comes to take me home.

Of course, my father shows me how to live out here. (And one day, I'll forget. Or I'll grow soft to that kind of living.) He teaches me to drive his beaten-up old trucks as soon as my eyeline can graze the top of any dashboard. He teaches me which peddles to press, and when, and why. He teaches me to pull over in the ditch so other cars can pass, and he asks me to trail him in his tractor. To pick him up where he has to leave it. He opens up the driver's door when I park. *Lookit that,* he says and smiles. *See, Bubba,* he says. *Easy.* And I scoot into the passenger seat so he can drive us home. Sometimes there are snakes in the road. Rattlesnakes, usually. The bullsnakes, he says, we leave alone, and my father teaches me the difference. (I couldn't say, now, what.) The rattlesnakes curl up and hiss and shake their chilling music. My father gets out from the truck—onto the empty road, what runs empty for miles—and pulls the garden hoe out from the back. I step out to watch him from a distance. I watch him lift the hoe and slam it down onto the road with a sudden spark to split the rattler, its body from its head. It's a commonplace motion out here: his mother does it, too, when we're driving in her small white car. When she sees a snake crossing. She goes back home for a hoe, or she happens to have one with her. And we children in the car watch her as she moves her body, white and thin and starting, then, to wrinkle, like bunched paper spread back flat. And she kills it in a single swipe. My father, he adds another swipe, and he reaches down to pick something up beside the corpse that twists its death reactions like a water hose set loose. He rubs the something against his jeans—small, and it smears a shade of purple on the denim—and he shakes it, and there's the sound of the snake holding to the space between us like an afterthought. My father walks to close the space. He puts the sound-maker in my palm, and I run a thumb against it. It's a texture, I think, like many hills—a contrast to this place my father raises me. I put it in my pocket.

Somewhere, for a long time, I had a box that carried all the rattlers my father ever gave me.

(I feel unsettled, sometimes, in everything I've left behind.)

I DON'T know what to do with my hands, how to stand. When the men chase down the cattle.

And I find that the cattle have been living near my early childhood memories. It's just the two of them: a mother and her calf, and when we pull up in my father's red truck, step out, I feel we've stepped into the past. The graying house is even more weather-stripped than before, and great piles of metal junk gather on the back porch. The chicken coop's dull honeycomb wiring has collapsed into itself, bent now in harsh curves into a yard of weeds where my father's several chicks and chickens once paced and pecked the ground. Tumbleweeds appear lodged, stuck, against the reddish fencing of the corral on the property's back end, where a donkey named Ol' Blue once wandered. Grandaddy's long-time farmhand lives here now, on-and-off, with his wife and kids and grandkids. They've returned to Mexico for the time being, he says, so what's here sits lonesome in its every place between visits.

No, my family's first house hasn't changed much: in fact, nothing much at all has changed—today, it just appears abandoned how we left it twenty years ago.

Pretty soon, they get the first one in the trailer: the mother. It's just her calf that's causing chaos. My father walks behind him with a tool that shakes, sounds almost like a rain stick. And the sound of sudden falling rain makes the young black calf jump and kick and ram into whatever's there ahead of him: first the closed rusting gate, and then the concrete trough where, as a kid, I caught, collected frogs, before the calf then slams against the metal curve of wall. Grandaddy stands back to watch my father chase the calf, the both of them kicking up some dust. And he's close enough to holler—to aid his son in spooking that small thing to find its mother.

I'm on the other side of the fence when the calf slams its child's weight against it. With an open palm, I'm smoothing out the wrinkles from my clothing as the calf's eyes bulge. As it breathes heavy through the fencing. Snot shoots out from its nose. Its back legs move in different directions than its front legs want to go, and the calf's wild anxiety makes me rub my hands hard against my jeans. To wipe them clean. To stick them down into my pockets. We stare long at one another as it struggles—until I break my stare to scan the ground for snakes. I step on empty patches between tight spots of brush and thorns and scattered cacti, and every step is light. As if I'm standing, walking, on my toes. As if the bottoms of my feet have chosen to rebel, but silent, with this earth.

"Aw," Grandaddy says, and it's drawn out where he stands, like a growl. "C'mon, now," and it's frustration. He pulls his hands away from where they cross along his chest to hold them, palms-up, like surrender. As if by will alone he might direct the panic toward a calm.

And the calf cries out. And I don't see snakes but cow shit: pale solid discs, and everywhere.

Then there's a clash, and I look up to see the calf has stumbled blindly into the trailer. Into its mother, who bellows out just as my father closes up the gate. He slips his gloves off, wads them up, and beats them hard against his boots. Soft clouds lift off and vanish as they do.

Just like the clouds of dust that trail us. That always do, out here, behind everything that moves. And back on the road toward town, my father has to steady the wheel to the sometimes shift of the trailer. To the movement of the cattle inside it. He has his own plot of land now, where he lives. He'll take them there, he says. They'll have it good. He's got his right wrist on the wheel so that his hand hangs over, steers us.

In the rearview's reflection, our old home shrinks to nothing until it's lost inside the dust.

Grandaddy's arm's an arch at the base of the passenger window. A thick finger brushes up against his top lip and rubs along his skin until he starts to yawn. He shakes his head and laughs. "Gettin' old," he says. He clips his words and runs them all together so they come out in a blend.

I sit in the backseat. Outside my window: rows and rows of budding plant in fields the same shade as my father's hands, his father's. A cloud of birds blooms up from out the cotton. And our passing has become, I think, a sort of disturbance out here. I watch the birds separate, fly off—land, and disappear. They settle, black, into that field of green and brown and speckled white.

Grandaddy clicks his tongue and shakes his head. "Time," he says. "It sure is crazy."

And he's smiling.

My father drives us in a crawl, and all those birds have landed somewhere far behind.

WHAT WE ARE

We know what we are, but know not what we may be.
—*HAMLET,* ACT 4, SCENE 5

(prologue)

Soliloquies meet static in my sister's girlhood springs. Boys in black hide hunched behind the backdrops of stretched bedsheets, their nervous shadows tapping mics to clear up avenues of sound. Women in headsets clutch clipboards, feed lines. Serve punishing looks. On a center stage of grass, a child Cleopatra pants against the aspic. *Poor venomous fool,* oh biting West Texas heat. A child Desdemona pinwheels every wild white limb until she, stone-still, lies smothered in her sweat. A child Ophelia drowns off-stage in a sea-salty gaze looking up. Looking out from that wet. Looking forth, we assume, to the sun.

(1.1)

It felt as if our parents always had a camera rolling. It's something that I'm thankful for: the fact that, somewhere, there exists a thousand marked and unmarked VHS tapes. Our archived memories. Somewhere, all that footage, I think, wherever it is, stays unwound. Somewhere, still, we're frozen in the doorway of that first house, and our mother has me wrapped up in a blanket, and she smiles at our father through the lens just as her heart turns, and he catches it. She kisses on my forehead, bunched, and leaves a wet spot. She rubs it with a thumb.

(1.2)

My sister's born, our parents say, a twister to my calm. A great wild nest of frizzy hair bounces through the house. Curls gather dust outside. She slams doors, shrieks for fun to fill up silence. One day, a hunched man nears her in the grocery store. *So cute,* he says, and smiles. Moves closer. Bends into her face. Our mother, when she tells it, laughs and says she sensed that it was coming. That she couldn't form the words to stop it quick enough: my sister's rearing back and slapping him so hard it rings out in the aisle.

(1.3)

Our father's 21 and full of booze and screaming out the lyrics of a song the party knows. Our mother's 19 and sees him with a beer raised to the ceiling of the living room. The fan spins on and on but can't thin out the heat. At least, this is how I imagine it. Our mother's plan: to leave her high school sweetheart. Our father's plan: to drop out, buy a plot of land, a barn. Convert it. To live with animals downstairs. Good thing, then, he sees her too. Good thing she makes, to him, the music stop.

(1.4)

I lie on my belly, on the ornate rug spread in the entryway of our second home, staring at the pedalboard of the lime-green piano pushed against the wall. The previous family's, left behind. Its keys look brown, or yellow, slightly lifted or else sunken in a row like ugly teeth. Lego pieces sprawl, lost, in all that carpet's twists and turns. On every Christmas morning, our father leans against an elbow on the rug and helps me build. Our finished castles line the perfect edge of the shelf beside my bed like an exhibition of a child's early OCD.

(1.5)

My sister has a silver microphone, a speaker. Her small voice carries through the crack beneath her bedroom door. She likes our father's Willie Nelson. The hallway's carpet rumbles to the tones, her dancing circles. Her jumping on and off her bed. Sometimes, we stage performances to Michael Jackson. To "Thriller." I flash the lights. We hide inside the closet just to leave it on a cue: to walk like zombies, to dance. I teach my sister where to go, how to move. How to make our parents laugh. How to make our mother laugh. Sometimes it's just our mother.

(1.6)

Our mother's almost 23 when she has me. Almost 27 when she has us. She steps around the house in search for anything to do. She keeps it clean, smelling like one of all the candles that I gift her every birthday. And our father, almost 30 at the arrival of my sister, is always planting cotton or pulling it. Sometimes I ride with him, and I read to him. Sometimes we take him lunch or dinner. Later, at the end of things, our mother will tell the both of us how she always dreamed of living in the Metroplex.

(interlude)

One year it's *Macbeth*. It's three young girls in ragged cloaks, prosthetic noses. My sister's classmates. The trio stand around a big black pot and squeal. Howl with laughter. The laughter's shrill, it's contagious, and so their parents laugh too. Say, *That's my kid.* Point laughing at Witch No. 3, *That's my kid.* The smell of hot dogs reeks, overwhelming from the sidelines. I tell myself that's what they're cooking, in their cauldron. And maybe they are. My sister sits behind that curtain, somewhere not far backstage. Another servant role. Our father looks to the grass. Our mother looks away.

(2.1)

I'm 12. An older cousin teaches me how to hide from parents. About clearing *history* and *cookies*. I'm 14. I talk with other boys like me online. We exchange common secrets. Descriptions of our changing bodies, of what we do to them. I'm 16. I talk with older boys like me online. Like the assistant children's basketball coach who says he wants to see me. Who I tell *Not yet*, before, *Okay*, but, *Not with sound*. When I'm sure I won't get caught, we masturbate together. And the laptop's bright, and off my face, and aimed right at my action.

(2.2)

My sister's growing gorgeous like our mother. She hides herself, she covers up in camo: head-to-toe. She wakes up early with our father on Thanksgiving. Watches him clean the rifles. It seems she's always at our father's side. They head out together, and they wait inside the blind. Their breath against the late November's freeze curls out in thin mists and mixes in the tight space between them. He teaches her to wait, patient. To lift the gun. To see whatever's seeing back inside the scope. Our father teaches her how to aim. To put her weight against the trigger.

(2.3)

Our father sees our mother's unhappiness. He sells his land. His cattle. His chickens. The life he'd built. Our family moves to Lubbock, Texas. To San Angelo, Texas. Our mother goes to work in speech rehabilitation. In hospitals. Our father goes to work climbing the white turbines that have begun to dot the landscape like Quixote's giants. One night, he shows us a picture at dinner. Of him, standing on the edge of things, a new kind of field behind

him: towers, spinning, harnessing the wind. He wears a harness.
He's attached to a cord. All in case he falls.

(2.4)

The night of a performance, only one I'll ever miss, I call the first
boy I ever thought I loved. Or maybe he calls me. His voice I don't
remember now, and really—how could I? 16 feels like a lifetime
ago. And anyway, it wasn't love. But I do draw circles round the
living room with my pacing, I do step up onto the fireplace and
back down onto the ground, I do balance on one leg in a heavy
lean against the kitchen's barstool backing. I do feel some weighted
inner workings of what I then called *love*.

(2.5)

My sister's a fighter. She switches schools when she gives the boy
who calls her *bitch* a bloody nose. She switches schools when she
gives the boy who calls her brother *faggot* an angry, purple bruise.
She calls me from bathrooms, panicked. Laughing. *Pick me up.*
One school aims to discipline. To instill lessons with Shakespeare.
Still, out of sight from teachers, her ears contain The Beatles. Len-
non. This, they say, is *sinful.* She rolls her eyes. She loses privileges.
I wish, I tell her one day, *that I were more like you.* So openly rebel-
lious, and proud of it.

(2.6)

Our father straddles the rooftop, calls out our mother's name. She
looks up from the flowers she beds in orange pots. Stands, pulls
away from dark earth. Shades her eyes from the sun's rays with a
hand. The other holds her waist. This, the one thing I know they
always did: Sunday trips to garden centers for seeds for tools for

mulch. The putting-down of color in our backyard. A time for par-
ent projects. He asks her for something, which she grabs. Which
she walks to the ladder. Which she climbs, which they exchange in
meeting, one the other, halfway.

(interlude)

One year it's *Romeo and Juliet*. Star-crossed lovers, Capulets and Montagues alive and dead in junior high. *Thus with a hug I die,* my sister mocks. Rolls her eyes. *A hug!* she says back then, at home, and laughs. *It's like they think we're* kids *or something.* My sister shakes her head. *A hug,* she says, but, still, she knows this truth: she is, in fact, a child. But her self-awareness is and always has been something else. I laugh. Our parents laugh. Because, we realize, the actors *are* just kids. All of them, out there. Playing bigger roles. Pretending.

(3.1)

I'm 17. The girl I've strung along has a cousin that's like me. He's visiting. One night, we sit beside her family's pool in pitch dark. Or we lie beside it, listening. Looking up at stars. Her cousin goes into the house and texts me: *Now?* I break away, inside. We make out on her bed. We mess her sheets. His mouth burns cool, like mint. And I'm 17. I sneak into another boy's room. I play for him on his keyboard, volume low. We close our eyes. Make out on his bed. I feel him growing through his jeans.

(3.2)

The child Cleopatra taught my sister how to want to kill herself. Or maybe that's not true. Maybe the want's innate, that it only needs to be encouraged. Whatever: Cleopatra's late-night message begs me to check. At my sister's bedroom door, down the hallway that connected us for years, I know I must knock. I don't remember. My memory can't vouch. And yet my old messages to Cleopatra say *it looked like she'd been crying.* That *she said her head hurt but she's okay.* That *I gave her a big hug and told her I'd see her in the morning.*

(3.3)

I don't remember when or where or why our father told us, just that he once alleged our mother's affair. Okay, the *why*: beer, beer, another beer after beer. His performance an avoidance of looks, lines delivered in a deadpan. This wasn't told that long ago, I should remember, and yet, the memory, like my father's speech, is slurred: our mother, he claims, snuck off, around, and time and time again, to see a man when we were young. A man, he claims, who had been our mother's high school sweetheart. A man his daughter would, in time, call *Dad*.

(3.4)
He's 21, in his parents' rental. I'm 18, senior year. The second boy I say I love. The first I ever really do. We won't last. I remember blue shag carpet burns along my back, a fast-slow rocking rhythm, first love I have inside me. Night drives around the lake, the edges of our town. We back into an auto shop and dent the building's corner. We pass my mother driving on the street, he ducks me down, and quick, to hide me in his lap. Until he gives the all-clear. Until we speed, laughing, back to that blue carpet.

(3.5)
My sister's caught one night with scissors in her hand. Kitchen cutters, baby blue handles. Kitchen cutters, slow to cut. My sister's caught, and when she is, she drops them. She cries. She screams at our mother, the catcher of everything. At least, this is how I imagine it. I think I'm asleep down the hallway. And the child Cleopatra, turns out, taught her this thing too. The cutting. Said it'd *make her feel alive.* Taught her how to steal laxative tablets, to take 4, 5 at a time. To *remain skinny.* Taught her how to think to *run away.*

(3.6)
When I've been caught telling the boy I loved *I love you* on the phone, our father closes off. Busies himself outside, on rooftops. Shoots arrows into targets by the pool. Our mother turns into a satellite. She orbits me, my room. Hangs in doorways in her pink plush bathrobe, arms crossed, eyes sad and red and dying. When I sneak out to see the boy I told *I love you,* she goes looking. Drives

up, down the streets. His neighborhood, like a cop. Speaks distraught into my voicemail and howls to root me out. Dog sniffing out scared rabbit.

(interlude)

One year it's *The Tempest*. The child Miranda runs to center stage in rags. She looks out to us, the audience. The storm on her horizon. She stands beside the child-wizard Prospero, his funny beard hanging tattered, white, and heavy from his face. *If by your art,* she says, *my dearest father,* in a voice like a squeak, *you have put the wild waters in this roar,* to the thunder-sounds my sister makes behind the curtain, behind the scene, *allay them!* I sit, leg shaking, beside our mother. Our father stands looking off, somewhere far beyond us and the crowd.

(4.1)

I'm 18. I smoke weed on the rooftop of my university's library. I don't get high, but the experience is enough. I kiss the boy who will become my second boyfriend on the rooftop of the parking garage. The third boy I'll say I love. The second I really do. I get high from this, more-so than before. He's from California, and this, ridiculous, feels exotic. We walk quick to my dorm. Hold steady in the elevator. We hurry down the hall. In my room, roommate gone, we shed our clothes like falling leaves. We catch each the other's breath.

(4.2)

My sister dates a boy who comes out to me. This is strange. She dates a country singer who shares my birthday to the year. This is strange. She dates a parachute rigger in the Army years older than her, a year older than me. This is strange. This ends in disaster. This ends in hate, and I overhear the end. When I walk back to our hotel room, I stop when I hear sounds of pleading through a cracked door. The *I love my brother.* The *I love you.* The *What does his sin have to do with me?*

(4.3)

I don't know what they did so near the end. When our father moved from their bed to mine. When our mother would have stopped saying *Love you,* stopped rolling over for that last day's kiss. It's near the end, the last chapter of their married life, when he tells me about Hawaii: the place she always wanted to go. How he booked a getaway for two, packed her bags and made arrangements for them both. How he showed up to pick her up, to get away. How her coworker came out instead to say, *I think you should go.*

(4.4)

California boy won't work. We near two years before love floun-
ders out, three before it dies. We're in his Texas apartment, red eyes
full of tears, and he says, *So.* Says, *That's it?* I make for the door,
and he wails. He wails and throws himself against it, me. He wets
my shirt. I think about the neighbors. He curls into himself and
says, *Please,* says, *Please stay,* says, *Please please stay.* And I do. To
make some sad form of love. Until the heat's worn off our naked
bodies. Then I dress. I say I'm sorry. And I go.

(4.5)

Bats collect at my sister's bedroom window. This, when she's left
our mother's house to find her own way. She'll describe this time
later as *lost.* Not *lost* as in *wasted* but *lost* like *unfound.* So when the
bats show up, who does she call? Our father? No. What, she might
think, can he do for me now? Is it our stepfather? Maybe. She's
started calling him *Dad.* This is strange. This is why our father slaps
her. This is why happy things end. I think, most likely, she just calls
the apartment management. Keeps her troubles far from us.

(4.6)

The day our mother remarries, our father's not far away. It rains.
Inside an old white wooden church in a remote West Texas town
called Buffalo Gap, I'm standing, waiting with my sister to walk
our mother down the aisle, when the music cuts in. A country
song on the groom's small speaker. Ten or so faces turn around and
stare, and, *This is it,* I realize: the walk to finalize our family. *What's
wrong?* my mother asks, just as we take the first step. I shake my
head. *Just don't talk,* my sister says. It rains until *I do.*

(interlude)

I surprise myself: I fall in love with Shakespeare in my senior year of college. I tell my sister about it, and she laughs. *Never,* she says. And her face bunches into wrinkles, and she smirks. *Never again.* I tell my mother. I tell my father. *Remember,* I say, *those performances?* And the both of them, in separate places now, they do the same thing with their faces. Their eyebrows lift. Their cheeks fill up with air just to release it all at once. *Remember?* they ask, and pause, and laugh, full, just like their daughter. *How could I forget?*

(5.1)

I find myself high in my best friend's bed. White sheets lift with us beneath. Eyes bear into the other's all seeing, suddenly, something different. His body smells like his smoke from the night before. I cry in my apartment. It's too soon after California. I'm 22. Later: constant sneaking to fuck, our friends left in the dark. I'm not sure, now, why we do this. Maybe to make a thing known is to lead it closer to its end. Or maybe the thrill of us is enough for us and us alone. Maybe no one ever needs to know.

(5.2)

Our mother's remarriage quickly falls apart. Our stepfather, that high school sweetheart, a study in sociopathology. He buys a brown bullmastiff puppy just short the size of terror. Our mother always keeps a clean house, and did. Until the puppy shits on the floor. Pisses in the hallway. Steps on, sits on, chews up her belongings. Later, when my sister goes to collect pieces of her bedroom left behind, she tells me what she sees. Shit, everywhere. Big puppy shit. Blinds ripped from the windows, chewed up on the floor. *You wouldn't believe,* she says, *that Mom ever lived there.*

(5.3)

The day our father remarries, our mother's not far away. It's in the country club of a familiar neighborhood. Small, just family. When he stumbles to the table where they've placed us, I tell him he looks handsome in his jacket. He laughs, tells us that he bought it months ago. For a funeral. They say their vows, and he walks to hug my sister. He holds her. Squeezes her. And he turns to hug me. *We'll be alright,* low in my ear. His voice catches in a choke. *We'll be alright.* They fly out to Hawaii in the morning.

(5.4)

But people know, they always will. When two people are in love. We live together in an apartment near the graveyard. We drop acid and watch fireflies near graves flash on and off and on again. Watch neon signs across the street flash off and on and off again. Until we move into a crooked house. Where we stray far from headboard by morning. Where something hangs at the backdoor, from before us. A small jar holding a bright blue stone, a human tooth, a shredded dollar bill. *Must keep something out,* we say. It stays there, just in case.

(5.5)

My sister runs away from home. From West Texas to the Metroplex. A kitten tears across the carpet of the new apartment she shares with a boy who's sweet on her. *Wild thing,* they say, and they laugh together. Talk turns to our parents, as it does. As the kitten runs around our feet. *Mom's always liked you more,* my sister says. I don't know what to say. *I was too wild.* The kitten climbs her legs, she winces. *Too much like her.* We all lived so close those years, I want to say, and somehow, still, so far away.

(5.6)

Our mother meets our father months before he gets remarried. This is what I know. That she steps into his truck. That he says he's sorry about how things went. With her new ex-husband, not the two of them. That they sit, engine running. Air blowing cool. Dashboard glowing dim, for hours. Much longer than they meant to. Until his fiancé's calling. Screaming, cursing through the phone. And when he hangs up and opens up the glove compartment, for what I can't remember, my mother sees the whiskey. A new-lit version of her longest lover. Our father, her best friend.

(epilogue)

Each year we sit in plastic folding chairs beneath a sprawling tent.
A celebration of the Bard behind my sister's private school. We sit
too close together, near melting in the heat. The fourth of us kneels
down somewhere up front. She plays the servant to her classmate
then, that child Cleopatra. Our father holds up the family camcorder. Our mother smiles small. I draw circles in my palm. The
electronic mimic of young voices buzzes through broken speakers,
a constant fading in-and-out. Their voices might carry some, but
soft, and not enough. They were, I realize now, just kids.

BAPTISM

The sunken light of our backyard's pool illuminates what's blue and shines just bright enough to hint at outlines in the bordering dark. I know, because I'm wrapped around another boy—arms squeezing round his neck—and staring, eyes half-open, past his shoulders: at the backside of my family's house. As he slips himself—a finger, working two—inside me, I see my father's wheelbarrow, off to the side of his shed and looking formless; and the ladder, his, that hugs the fence. My mother's ornate cross stands, too, among the ivy, almost, I think, with this boy's breath hot on my neck, like a warning. And I'm too afraid to close my eyes, because I fear that I might open them to something new: my mother or my father or my younger sister, standing in the windows to the living room. Or worse: my family standing on the edge of things, in the almost dark.

I'm afraid, I think, in retrospect, I'll see my father standing with a gun.

I'm 19 and home from college for the summer. This boy, he's just flown in from California, and my mother, she's just entered the final stage of grief: *Acceptance.* She's allowed for this visit to happen, regardless of my father's bedroom protesting, because she's trying to be better now. *No, really,* she says, with the hope of eclipsing that which came before. *I'd really like to meet him.* My father, meanwhile, drops his eyes, his voice; he sulks through the rooms and hallways of our home. His clear resistance grinds against the rest of us: conform to change, we say—in many ways, unspoken— or else get left behind.

Of course, even up to now I've never seen the active violence of my father. Only what's been left in his wake: a hole punched in his closet door that my parents never patched up. It stares at me from down the hall—my father's closed-door reply to my coming-out.

It holds as an image in my mind. It keeps my eyes from shutting all the way. And as I breathe out, warm, into California's ear, I press my temple close to his—and beads of water mix with the beads of our sweat: clear and indistinguishable apart, milky joined together. I kiss what's gathered on his skin and feel his forehead wet my lips. Taste his salt—catch my eyes and stare ahead, behind him.

The heat's a dry one here, in San Angelo, Texas, and the nights are heavy with it. Though I can't know it yet, it's the last summer I'll ever have in this town. In this house, this pool. With the fountain that waterfalls straight down into the middle of that shining blue, and the neighbor's dogs in the alley behind us that run and bark like wild worship at night sirens. But there are other sounds too: that water from the fountain, falling on, into, itself, and the crickets in the fresh-cut grass, and those late-night drivers on the road along the frontside of the house, each passing by like welcome wind. And here, a breeze is rare: and when it whispers through the backyard, the bunched leaves of the bushes and the ivy on the fence shake and sound almost like footsteps.

And then, tonight, there's us: the disturbance. The water's tides; what breaks those tides.

We'd waited in my bedroom for the all-clear of the house's silence. I'd pushed my bedroom door against itself and turned the handle—slowly, turned the handle—and pulled it, gentle. Swung it open toward us. Quiet. In nothing but our swim trunks, we'd walked with bare and careful steps together down the hallway. And mine: bold red and holding just a step above mid-thigh, I'd felt next-to-naked in them—like pure sex—and *confident* beside him. At the end of the hallway, just as California turned ahead of me, I turned to look behind: at the doorway to my parents' room, open like a mouth's long gape. Like something waiting, alive. With nothing but black on its other side—and that closet door, its wound unseen, staring back at me. Once outside the house, we'd quickened both our paces. We'd stepped over the pool's blue net, what my father had used to clean it—the pool: his passion project—just earlier that day. We'd toed the water. Pulled back and made a sucking sound through teeth. Laughed and stared at one another, at hair and goosebumps rising on our arms, with our eyes wide and ready. We'd both stepped in together: and the pool ate, first, our feet and then our ankles; it pasted all the dark hair to our legs and rose and entered past our thighs to fill our swim trunks. And the water formed itself around what bulged inside those shorts as we'd entered to our necks, as we'd both kept pulling at the fabric from its sticking to our skin. Until he'd slipped his down to ring around his feet, and I did the same. And our shorts came floating up so that we had to catch them—to leave them floating near the steps, bunched together, hiding just below the pool's rounded lip.

And now, California fingers me beneath the water. And with my eyes closing—quickly, giving in—I find that I can't help it: I think about a man's propensity for violence. At the end of things, when faced with sudden change. When pushed against a wall. And as California fingers me, my hand falls from his back to grip the pool's edge, the surface that rounds it, and it's rough, and it leaves the imprints of small dots along my skin. And I think of inheritance: the things we carry from one place to another: like old rifles, stacked in bags and laid-out like dead bodies underneath the house. What's pointed to in some old memory—*Don't touch*—and closed away with a square of carpet that fits into the closet floor.

I don't listen to the memory voice. I lean back as California feels around inside of me. I run both of my hands down his chest, his dark hair, what's vast and all along his front, and I smile—grab his working hand and pull it, slow, until he's out of me: and I let a sound escape like punctuation, and we kiss. His tongue runs up to mine, and I feel the edges of his teeth and the soft of inner cheek. I bite his bottom lip and suck and let him go. I hook my eyes to his so that it's only him and only me—so that there's nothing but the pool—and I hold my breath. I climb down his body, down until my head is underwater. I taste the bitterness of the water before I have him in my mouth. I feel him growing, hard, and taste a certain sweetness on my tongue. And I look: to watch the hair around this part of him wave, slow, like black and tangled seaweed, before I close them fast—my eyes—because the chlorine stings. I feel a burn behind them, and I grip his backside, tight, to anchor, bob my head, slow—faster, until it's all I'm thinking of: that burn. Until I feel my eyes are open even as they're shut. And when I have to breathe, I climb back up his body, and I inhale: something heavy, quick, and quiet, and I run both hands along my head to slick the water from my hair. It falls in drops to patter on the sur- face. I open my eyes, I blink them. Until the burning's gone, away, or going. I laugh low between us like a secret as he smiles—California—as he pulls me close against his body. As he stares into me, prepares me and himself below the water.

And he lets out something like a sigh, and drawn out, as he enters me. He closes his eyes at the breach as mine roll back—when I open my mouth and rear my head as if for air and grip at the skin of his shoulders—and he shakes his head, slow, and, under breath, he, *Fuck,* he says. He says, *Fuck,* and he smiles as we rock together. As waves crash against the edges of the pool, as they slap against our skin, disturb our gathered swimsuits, floating. And I feel it on my mouth—his smile, between the *Fucks*—when I open my eyes again. To stare over his shoulder and back into the dark. To the wheelbarrow and the ladder and the garden's cross covered to its tips in ivy.

And there's the sound like footsteps, and the touch of breeze against droplets on my neck.

And in the back of my mind, I see something else: the outline of a figure—a familiar figure in the dark, a man—standing tall beside the bushes. Holding onto something at its side. Lifting that something up. Aiming: and my face contorts to knowing when *a sudden flash* of blue edged white rips a hole into the dark, and it's a punch, an asterisk, that's bright and bold and powerful. My hands release his skin, lift up, too late, to shield my eyes from such an awful suddenness, and my ears, they both ring echoes as I jolt back, fast, away, like I've been shot, just as the boy I'm wrapped around—the one who pulses like a reflex, still inside of me—his head, it bounces forward, *slams* against my chest. I open my eyes, and I look down, and I suck in air: once*twice*—two sudden things, like I'd forgotten this whole time to come back up. Like my head, with the rest of me, is still underwater—hearing, *seeing,* underwater—and all I see is red: red water all around me, pluming up: red splatters on pale skin: a red emptiness in front of me where before there was a smile, and *pieces* floating where they shouldn't.

I'm close, he whispers, and it's enough to bring me back. To the water's slap, to his skin on mine. To the wiry brush of his hair. The wheelbarrow, and the ladder, and the garden's cross, each dull and lonely in the dark. And our tangled bodies block the pool's sunken light to cast shadows of ourselves that stretch and merge along the bottom of it. Our shadows climb the opposite wall until they can't, and then they're stuck to here—this place, this perfect blue—like me to him. I stare beyond us, at the sharp reflection of the light in my family's house's windows. I know that I won't tell him what I've seen, or that I see it all the time. That I worry, here, and everywhere. That this pool, that California, can't contain the fear, not really.

Instead, I moan, I bite his ear. Until his nails leave marks with sudden grips into my back.

I moan and rock my body pressed to his. I watch for movement in the dark.

AXIS

He's rounding a curve, crushing a can, setting the just-bent form in a cupholder. White dust blossoms out from behind us, behind his big red truck, kicked up by tires that transition from this—the dirt road jutting off the main one, leading to the Llano State Park campsite and true Texas Hill Country—onto the highway, to black tar. It's a smooth welcome. He's turning, no blinker, but it's fine: no one's out, and it's getting late. He reaches back, eyes still on the road ahead. Reaching 50, 55, 60—75, and coasting.

It's our father, driving, my sister in the back, me up front, playing passenger. We're on our way into town, and he's reaching.

Let me get it, I say, not knowing what to get but turning to help out anyway. I'm a year out of college and back from a job overseas. I'm here because my father planned this trip months ago: an escape in his camper, just the three of us. My sister, nearly four years younger and fresh out of school herself, sits in the back and stares at nothing out the window. She plays with her hair. When I turn around, she looks at me, eyebrows lifted. She looks down at his searching hand. She knows—we know—he's reaching for the bright red and white cooler there behind my seat. *Let me get it,* I say again, and I ask him what he's reaching for. My sister turns back to the window.

Our father pauses. He seems embarrassed, and maybe he is. I think he is. Like a kid, caught. *Oh,* he starts, and stops reaching. He pulls back, puts the reaching hand up to his mouth. He draws a quick circle with his thumb and index around his mouth, along the graying hair there. He places both hands back on the wheel. Sniffs. *Another beer,* he says, and he speaks as if delivering a joke.

As if, *Knock knock?*

As if, *Who's there?*

As if, *Alcoholic father.*

And I laugh something quick. I laugh, I think, because I feel sorry.

You can't, I say. *You can't do that. Sorry.*

I say sorry.

Not when we're in the car.

And.

I mean, not ever.

But.

Not when we're in the car.

His response is mocking. Playful. And, I know, subdued. *Aw, c'mon now.* He glances up into the rearview, into the driver-side mirror's empty reflection. He changes lanes. He asks if I want a beer. I say no, and he laughs. *Aw,* he says, and he draws this one out. His nose—tanned near-brown like his father's, from a lifetime of sun—it suddenly twitches to scratch, I think, at some inner itch. *Awright.* He glances, for a moment, not back into the mirror on his door but to the scenery beyond it: the blur of a dried yellow ditch, cracked wooden fenceposts and barbed wire, unending mesquite.

At times I catch my father looking off like this, locked in. Gone, for just that moment.

I say sorry. I feel a sudden heat rise up in my cheeks, in the pits of both my arms. I look ahead and count the yellow stripes that pass beneath us on the highway. I focus on one distant one at a time, pull it closer with my looking. I put a leg underneath me, rock forward to adjust, and I sit like this. Like a child. And this, I think, is why my father drives, why I allow him to drive: he is still my father, and I am still his son. I count the stripes until I forget. Until I have to start again. Until the sun starts its slow reaching for the earth, the moon for the sky.

At the gas station he asks us what we want. *Anything?* I say chocolate, but he says there's already some back at the campsite, in the camper. For the fire we'll build, later. For s'mores. But he jumps on my sister's request. (Whatever it was, I can't remember—though maybe the thing itself doesn't matter, not really.) He's stepping out, putting the nozzle in the side of the truck. Letting the gas pump itself as he walks inside the station. And we talk about this new father, who I haven't seen in a year, who my sister hasn't spoken to in nearly two. About how much he's changed. That wiry, untouched hair around his mouth like outward evidence. About this, his new addiction: dependence on drink, and, maybe, on needing company. When he comes back, he comes back holding a chocolate bar. *Just in case,* he says, and he sets it down between us. He starts the engine. Passes back whatever it was he grabbed for my sister. She thanks him, and we return to silence.

It's a McDonald's dinner. The reason for this short trip into town. In the drive-thru, my father calls the employee by her name. She's my age, maybe a year or two older. Twenty-five or twenty-six. Heavy-set, not that it matters. Our father is loud and flirtatious. We don't think he knows this, or maybe he does: maybe it's a mechanism, a showing-off, and why? Because he's doing okay, and I think he wants us to know this.

That he's doing okay. He is. He insists that he is.

And he's nearing concern as we drive back, when I'm not eating the chocolate bar. It sits there on the center console like a trap. I explain I'm saving it for later and he nods, his right hand—work-dirty and calloused—a loose grip at the wheel, his elbow resting at the window. I touch the chocolate bar where its heart might be until it presses, soft, under my thumb. Like us, it submits to the heat.

We're cruising, back at 75, 80. The truck's bright beams pierce the night.

There are no other lights out here to guide us.

WHEN WE'RE three hours late showing up to the kayak rental the next morning, our father simply waves his hand.

Aw, he says, the black wad of dip a lump in his bottom lip. *It's no problem.* His speech rolls out slightly muffled by the lump, and I think of a father (our father, the father of childhood) returning to this old habit with no one, now, to speak against it. And I think of our mother's once-vocal disapproval as he spits, careful, into a Styrofoam cup before he sets it back beside him. Before he grips the wheel again. And the spit slides down the cup's curved walls to stain the insides yellow.

When we pull up to the building—a facade like a Wild West general store, a welcome sign pocked with fabricated bullet holes—it's two guys my age sitting on the porch outside. Baseball caps and sunglasses. They turn to watch our approach. They crush their cans of Coke and put endings to their stories. Stand to greet. My father steps out of the truck but leaves it running. *Should I do any-thing?* I ask. Meaning, *Need help?* But my father, he waves his hand again. *Aw, naw.* Furrows his brow and sniffs. *You're good, man.* He shuts the door. He walks right up to the porch, and my sister and I watch him from inside the truck. I see my father shake their hands, strong, firm—I can tell because it's in the rigid way their elbows shift midair, the slight hovering. There's laughing. A shaking of heads. One of the guys, the alpha—tan and taller than his friend, head buzzed and golden under his hat, t-shirt, jeans, Confederate belt buckle—he points to the other side of the shop. Moves his index around in front of him like he's giving directions. He says something to accompany this, but all I hear is the low hum of his speech through the windows. A depth. My father's nodding, and he's walking back, as the alpha and his friend move off in the direction of the former's previous gesture. They climb into a truck with red and yellow kayaks stacked tall on a trailer behind it. And my father, he's getting back into his own truck, reversing. Ready to follow.

Was it okay? I ask. Meaning, *Being so late?*

Aw, yeah, my father says, and he follows right behind them, onto the highway. *No problem.*

An easy 20 minutes out of town, we park the truck where the river will later spit us out. *We'll leave the truck here,* our father tells us. *Ride the rest of the way up-river with them.*

So I step out. My sister steps out. My father steps out, but he's slower, doing something, always working his hands. I start toward this other truck. I'm wearing swim shoes—*river shoes,* my father calls them, as he often does when he suggests I buy a cheap pair and bring them out on trips like this—and I'm wearing those old red swim shorts—bold, bright red, near neon in the sunlight, the ones that end well above my knees, my pale legs, thighs—and I'm self-conscious. I cover myself with the cooler I lug ahead of me, full of the waters and beers and snacks my father thought to bring.

I open the back door. The alpha's driving. The other guy, same build, same white skin, West Texas twang, he sits in the passenger seat. Both have on their sunglasses, so I can't see their eyes. Their features. What they must be thinking, or the truth in their stares.

Hey, I say, knowing that's a universal start. *Thanks for driving us.*

Aw, the alpha says in a drawl, sounding more like my father than I do. *No problem.*

I scoot in, and my sister follows right behind. The four of us watch my father at his truck. *What is he doing,* my sister says, after a while of watching. The guys up front laugh. *He's always moving slow,* I say. And I'm conscious of the way I keep my voice set to a lower pitch than what's usual. And I think I force my father's drawl. But the guys up front, they just go on laughing. *He takes his time,* I say. *Seems like it,* the alpha says in return. We watch my father spit brown into a cup; we watch as he puts the cup in his truck, locks it up; we watch as he reloads himself, pulling out the small, rounded tin from his shirt's front pocket containing the dip—a dark mass he grips with his right forefinger and his thumb, lifts, and casually places between lower lip and gum. He returns the container to indent its place just above his heart, and only then does he really start moving.

And when our father's back with us, we're driving off. I let them do all the talking—these other guys and my father—because they talk the river: of the park itself and its wild game; what it's like in the summertime, the best spots along the way, the worst when the river's so low from drought as it is now; about the groups that make it out here: big groups—the families. They talk and laugh, and I keep my hands splayed wide over my knees, my naked thighs, desperately wishing to cover up the stark-white skin, wondering why I wore these shorts in the first place.

I see the signs we pass of warning, of *Fire Danger,* with their arrows aimed at red.

When we're dropped off, the guys leave us with hopes for good times on the water. Tell us that the ride back down shouldn't be any more than 5 hours, though my father, he insists it won't be any more than 4. They laugh and shake on it—a sort of punctuation out here—and we're alone again: my sister, my father, and me, with nothing else but the river and the sound of its running. We pull our kayaks alongside us and get in.

THE WATER is low, as we were warned. Much lower than usual. When I overturn, it's because the water's picked up speed; or else because the kayak's hit a tall-standing stone; or else because of a stream-dividing tree, its branches merciless and whipping at the skin of arms that lift to hide my face.

When this happens, when I overturn, my sister laughs and passes right along. She's pulled her hair up and out of her face so that it sticks out at odd angles from its tight knot, and I think of our mother, the way she'd always put it up *just like that* on trips like this, near water, her hair the same shade of dark. We're a quarter down the river now, or else halfway, but there's no way of us knowing. Our time out here marks itself as the heat on our shoulders, the introduction of color on our bodies. My sister cups water from the river and pours it onto her legs. She makes a habit of this so that, this far down the river, I think she's hardly aware of her motion—from cooling water to skin and back again.

When this happens, when I overturn, our father's too far back and around a corner to see. I stand, current-trapped but laughing. I wish to flip the kayak back onto its red underbelly before my father passes—this isn't something that would happen to him, I think. But he shoots around the bend, glides along like this, just like my sister. Just like his daughter. *Okay?* he asks, moving farther and farther away. I watch him hit a rough spot, bounce. Stay upright. He goes on, laughing too.

The better part of the float is smooth, like the river, the Llano, cut between cliffsides and yellowing slopes and run-down docks. We pass rope-swings in trees and private property, *No Trespassing,* and cautious deer and heron and turtles on logs that dip quickly into the water like skipped stones when we pass. My sister and I collect odd leaves or the occasional pecan or small branch aimlessly drifting along, and when we reach with an extended oar to pick these up, we dump them on the other's kayak in a strange and simple exchange. In the moments the three of us move close as a trio, I watch my father listen, watch his face light up when my sister speaks, watch his body shake with the full force of his laughter. At the low points of the float, I feel the roughness of long-buried rock and its kin grind along beneath me, and we often stand to set our courses straight.

My father brings this up, the river's level, again and again. He apologizes for it (again and again). He insists that it's not usually this way. That last time, he says—when he brought his girlfriend out, his brother and his brother's new wife—the rapids were *rapids,* and the river ran a course not requiring near as much work. No strain in the forward movement. Maybe, he says, we should come back, another time. When the river's not so low like this.

But my sister and I float on, of course, not caring, and telling him so. My father, it seems, bears the weight of worry for all of us. It's unnecessary, we insist, but he goes on talking (again and again) about the river's faults. Though I know his real worry has nothing to do with the river and yet everything to do with it: that his real worry is in losing us again, and in believing that the slow-crawling river might just be what finally takes us away for good.

How's it been? I ask my sister when we're alone, as if I haven't been here, on this same trip. Our kayaks bump and settle, and the sound they make is empty. They run together as a pair thanks to the oars we reach out, reach for and grab, that we pull until we're close. Our father's somewhere lost behind us, and we slow ourselves to let him catch back up. *You good?*

She smiles. Her brows, like our boats, pull close. *Fine,* she says. *Yeah, I'm fine.* She turns, looks over her shoulder, just as the front of our father's kayak peeks around a bend. He's still far enough away. *It's weird.* She turns back to look ahead. *It's weird.* And she laughs, shakes her head. *I don't know.*

And I don't doubt it. Sometimes I try to imagine some similar feeling, as if losing the father I knew from before all this isn't, somehow, enough. He's our father, I remind myself; he's *ours.* But it's different, and I know this—I've known this: that he and my sister live in this world as equals. Or, that they once did. That she grew up as an extension of our father, just as I did our mother.

I love him, she says. *Of course I love him,* as if convincing me, herself. She looks to her legs, cups water from beside our boats and cools them. *It'll just take some time to fix us.*

Something pokes its head above the water nearby, and then it plunges, disappears.

Is that what you want? I ask. *To be fixed?*

My sister quiets as our father nears, shrugs small. *I'm here.*

At some point along the stretch, when the river's width has grown and grown until the distance between shores requires two turns of the head to bridge them, it's just him—my father—and me; my sister floats on far ahead, near the coming rapids that churn the low water white. I watch my father as he empties his beer in one final tilt up and dips the empty can into the water. He fills it, pours it out. Shakes out the excess. He crushes the can and reaches out for that red and white cooler that floats alongside him, wedged in a tube and tied to his kayak with a rope. He drops can into cooler and pulls out another. Offers me one. I accept. In the exchange between us there's a flash of light, a sunburst born on a metal rim. In my hand the can is cool. I place the can between my legs and feel that same coolness drain in the heat of my thighs. My father shuts the cooler and lets it float a small distance away, as much as the rope allows. The sound of two cans opening—first one, a pause, and then the other—disrupts the stillness; the sound is, itself, *crisp.* He gulps and I sip.

What're you thinkin' of doin'? he asks after some natural silence—the hollow echo of a breeze we all wish to be greater, our boats on the water. I'm unemployed, taking what I call *a break,* unsure of what's next but not wanting to say so. *I'll take it easy,* I say. I paddle, glide. Hold my hand out to etch an uneven line over the water's surface. *Y'know,* he starts, *I think you'd really like*—and I know where this is going, and I know that he means well. *Dental tech.* That's the go-to, the buzzword job. Always has been. There's money in that. Or else: because he doesn't know what I do, that I write—or, he does, but not like this, not about *him* and *us*; not the secrets that we barely even tell ourselves.

I've published, I say out-loud, and for the first time to my father. *I did a reading, just last year.*

He sniffs. *Aw, that's cool, man.* Lifts his beer and sips. *Naw, that's cool.*

And we leave it at that.

He drinks as we float, and we float on together.

AT NIGHT, the fire crackles behind us like something mad slowly waking, coming to life. The lamp, battery-powered and set in the card table's center, distorts our features; it gives shadows a place to play on the sides of the camper, a reason to. We sit in red chairs with cupholder netting, the ones that fold in on themselves, that fit into bags and lie one beside the other beside the other on their off days in the back of my father's truck. The wall of trees behind the camper looms tall. Their tops cut a dark and jagged line into the night that sways as some subtle yet constant sort of reminder, and when we hear hushed rustlings in the tall grass at this wall's edge, we pause. We pause long enough for the grass to part like a curtain, for the armadillo to amble out, slowly. To watch us, halfway between its wooded world and our more open one. We joke about this armored creature, our state mammal, so rarely seen beyond roadkill. We laugh to match the night—a thing so soft between us—and the armadillo retreats from our sudden sound. We hear its escape. Its stirring. The grass parting or else collapsing before it, and I wonder at its fear: the threat of us.

Silence settles over. Wood pops, splinters in the firepit.

And when my father speaks, there's an underlying sadness. This isn't new. And it's not exclusive to the dark. Whatever it is that takes over our father, it hangs onto every word these days, manifests itself in the way tears settle, unformed—unbroken—and constant, at the base of his stare. But he is, I think. We think, my sister and I. Broken, I mean. Just a bit, if you can be.

Maybe, I think—every time, I think—he's yet to find his footing.

(But he's doing okay. He is. He insists that he is.)

And the night's a slow-burn conversation. A gateway to family tragedy. To our parents. What comes from it isn't new; in fact, it's too familiar. Expected, now.

How's your mother?

She's fine, we say. Happy, we lie.

That's good. He sips. Slurs. And, suddenly, *I miss her.*

We don't admit to knowing this. Three years now, just about.

I miss her every day. He shakes his head, a slow shake. He sips. Looks to the fire. *Every day.*

Another close rustling. Firewood collapsing in the pit. The voices of a group, their laughter, from another lot nearby but far enough away.

But I can't, he says, as suddenly as he missed her. His eyes look lazy to the fire. *Can't go back to that.*

To *that,* we think: the Easter Sunday brunch, the reaching for my mother's hand. The rejection of this act. The quiet tone his voice would carry, like a pleading, like a begging her *not this.* The move from bedroom to son's room to the living room couch. The move to a nephew's spare bedroom just down the street, a (world) neighborhood away from his house, his (old) home. The discovery of a new man, a man he knew, the high school sweetheart, and the truck parked in the driveway. The gun he carried, the late cir-

cles he drove around his (old) home. The searching for the truck.
The fantasies that played out, the list of punishments he planned:
this new man's image pinned to this (old) home's front door by
butcher knife, a shotgun, suicide in his wife's car, a closed garage.
The meetings with his daughter and the telling her these fantasies.
The getting drunk at restaurants. The meetings where he heard too
much, where his daughter slipped (or spoke out in defiance?) and
called the new man *Dad.* The parking lot slap, his daughter says
(and he denies)—the only time he'd ever struck one of his children in such a way—that ended them. The wanting, on his part,
to forget. The turning to forgetting. The fleeing to an unfinished
farmhouse in the country on a good friend's insistence. The good
friend's house a graveyard, then, for couches, big holes like moon
craters in the floor. The snakes like solid apparitions rising up in
summer heat to rest inside the kitchen, the bathroom, behind the
bedroom door. The back and forth and back to work. The fixing-
up the good friend's house, and the camper in the meantime. The
drunken rides on dirt bikes through the canyon with no helmet.
The rising speed, the reaching for it. The learning of his (ex-)wife's
wedding such a short time later. The rain he never saw, the country chapel. His son and daughter's grieving it all. (The day I know
lives on and on and warped within his head.) The dinner date
that someone soon set up, and the meeting of a short and sweet
blonde country girl, his (ex-)wife's perfect opposite. The short and
sweet blonde country girl herself so newly formed by sadness. The
moving out of the good friend's house, the camper. The staying in
the short and sweet blonde country girl's son's old bedroom. (The
staying, we knew and didn't care, in hers.) The growing of hair
on chin, on upper lip. The changing of a man. The acceptance
of a life with short and sweet blonde country girl. Companion-

ship. The feasting, reciprocal, one on the other's sadness. And all
the parties that they'd throw. And all the parties that they'd go to.
The driving through a good friend's house on that reckless canyon
dirt bike, and the drinking with the neighbors' kids. The weekend trips to Mexico, and the AC/DC backyard cover bands, and
the endless state of blacking out, of being. The calls he'd make to
his son, his only, who'd been far away from it all. (Who had run
away from home—as it seemed, then, to the son and, maybe, to
his family—to school, then to another country, overseas—as they
fell apart.) The speaking of his (old) life, his (ex-)wife, on these
calls. The short bursts of sobs into the phone. The apologies. The
asking about his son, and yet, not really. The formality of asking.
And the hanging up. The driving to a plot of land just down the
road from short and sweet blonde country girl's home, his new
one. The quiet field. The tractor that he bought, and all the chickens, and the cattle. The trenches drawn so deep into the soil, and
the planting of new seed. The waiting for rain. The therapy, his
therapy he said worked better than any talking ever could: the
silence out there, and this breaking of the earth. The holding tight
to something familiar—the cotton farmer self. The remnants of a
life before, identity reclaimed.

   The glow of the campfire burns against the edges of our bodies, and it flickers shadows on our features. Nearby but just outside of the glow, the taillights of my father's truck reflect the fire's
light, and low, like the red eyes of something waiting. *I don't like to
bring up*—and our father pauses, and his mouth hangs open, just
slightly, like a trout land-trapped and struggling to breathe—*the
bad.* He looks down at the beer in his hand. He rotates the can.
And it must feel cool where it rests, I think, in the dip between fingers. He sniffs, and there's the sound of his sipping. My sister looks

to the ground. She makes small shapes in the air with her feet, and I watch her as she does this: fluid motions hovering just above the earth, a figure-eight, her leg a pendulum swinging back and forth.

Our father looks off into that darkness bordering the campsite. The fire burns low, and its light does not allow the darkness its full nature; instead, the night around us appears infected, to some degree, with a dimness. And in the dimness: some static quality. A holding-back.

We acknowledge, in this, our great shift.

And we talk until the fire dies into itself. Until the small things in the brush start moving back toward camp and something cries out in the distance. Screams, from far away. This silences us. This has us all looking back to the tree line. Beyond it. It's the calling-out of some breed of deer, our father says, or something like it. He tells us what it's called, but I soon forget. A *deer*, he says, though it sounds like a woman. A woman *screaming*, I think, from up in the hills or somewhere closer, near the river. My sister calls it creepy. My father thinks it's beautiful. And maybe it is. Beautiful.

(It's much later on when I look it up, find it again: the *axis deer*, nonnative to this country.)

When the talk dies and we head back inside, to the camper, I watch as my father makes a space for us to sleep. I watch as he shoves the sheets down into the corners of my sister's bed, tucks them under the sides. I watch my father, *father*. Step over himself, stumble, slightly. He gets down to his knees where my sister and I sit up on opposite beds. *Awright*, he says, and he reaches for his children's hands. I settle my palm into his, the other into my sister's, and my father holds on tight. My sister does too. And, like our mother, since the divorce, our father's left the church—but he prays, here, just like we used to do, as a family. Just like he has—he tells us—every night since that other time, before. His comfort, I realize—eyes closed, head bowed—has, at some point, become my discomfort. And when it's over, he squeezes on the *Amen.* He kisses my sister on her forehead, kisses me on mine. His breath smells sweet, smells sour. *Love you guys.* He walks toward the camper's other half. Clicks off the light. *Glad you're here.* The camper shakes as he rocks back into the darkness, to the place where he sleeps; where he'd slept at the end of a marriage, of a life as he knew it.

Family, scattered.

Crickets chirp low to the deer's screaming in the hills. The heat is heavy, still.

BLURS

Sweltering air. 7-Eleven. I sweat inside my hoodie. From all the waiting and the heat that pushes out through vents above me. The inside of the store's glass facade steams white so that I can't see much beyond it. Where it's late December, and the gray roads color orange from every lonely light above them. Inside, the man behind the counter hunches over where he stands. He has a big dark mole on his lip. Brown skin. Thick black hair all up and down his arms. He doesn't smile. Doesn't speak. He lets the bright green numbers on the register speak for him. The man in line in front of me stands tall. Looms large. Like someone's Army dad that I once knew. He doesn't smile. He has bright pink sausage fingers that hold his money at his waist. A thick gray mustache that weights the features of his face. And a drawl like Abilene, Texas. Like twenty miles south of it, or some place called Tuscola. Like a Larry McMurtry story. He asks the man behind the counter for a lottery ticket. He points at a roll behind the clear thick plastic divide and gives a peace sign. "Two." There's the sound of checking out—the sound of late-night radio—the sound of the front door opening again. The door's chime. A woman rushing in from outside bundles to herself. She blurs, gone and down an aisle before I can see her much at all. I push my hands inside my pockets. The door closes, and it closes like a heartache: slow. A drawn-out thing. Like the half-end of a yawn. And through the doorway—brief—I see my sister's car outside and the clouded windows and her, looking up and locking eyes. The outside finds its way inside enough to feel its stay, and the door shuts with its sigh. And the yellow candy wrappers, and the red candy wrappers, and the silver candy wrappers in the display on the counter shake in-place. And the song changes on the radio, and it's a Christmas song. And it's late. And the looming man in front of me takes both his tickets. He steps away as I step up. I pretend to know exactly what I'm doing as I point behind the man behind the counter. "Marlboro." (I like it, if I'm being honest, for its red-and-white.) He asks for my ID, and I confirm it: 23. He scans the pack, and the machine beeps shrill at us. I hand off my card, and I hear the chime and feel the outside step back in. I turn to watch the tall mustached man's back before he's out of frame, behind the window's haze, and my sister in her car stares down at something just below the steering wheel. I watch her as the door sighs. As the woman from before steps up behind me. Not so much a woman, I think, but a girl. My sister's age, like 19, and she radiates perfume. She wears a summer dress. White florals on a stretch of black. And a thick blue winter jacket. Tan cowgirl boots. She leans from one foot to the other, cradling a gray six-pack of beer in the space just below her chest. The man behind the counter nods at me as if to say I'm good, and I slide the pack of cigarettes back toward myself along the counter. "Thanks." I step away. The cowgirl steps up to the counter, and I step outside. The door chimes. And I feel the night air rush inside my jacket, the hair along my arms stand up. It's sudden, how I'm cold again. The gas station warmth melts off me like an ice cream's starting sweat, and I hear the door's last sigh. Inside my sister's car, I shiver. Blow warmth into cupped palms. (I'm loud about it.) "Fuck." And I laugh. "Fucking *cold.*" But it doesn't stay that way, because the heater's been on, long. My body finds it can't adjust to all the back-and-forth. And I feel my body's thawing out, again. Like I might puddle on the floorboard. But I don't, and my sister's turning on her headlights. Backing up. The double lights shine bright against the storefront, widen out. Slide slow along the building. They turn to face the road where lights dot plots of orange until they don't. Until it's just my sister's headlights speeding into nothing. "You see that girl?" my sister asks. Her tone, not too far from the song that's playing on her radio. (Slight country. Lost and looking.) "Cowgirl boots?" I ask. And my sister nods. "Yeah, well," and her eyebrows arch. And her nose lifts. "She's a *bitch,*" she says, and I laugh. My sister laughs. And the woman on the radio gives up to fiddle. To an interlude that sounds a lot like what's out here. The ditches that rise up to thick mesquite on either side of a backroad. The flimsy barbed wire fences. "How do you know that?" I ask. And the smoother road transitions to a rougher one. A light haze of dust hangs in the air before the headlights. "Used to see her out a lot," my sister says. "At parties." (And I imagine what my sister's like at parties. How much it is she drinks. What it is she drinks the most of. How she stumbles room-to-room in seeking-out some conver-sation, or *if* she does, like me.) Apparently, she says, the cowgirl cheated on her ex with someone from another school. (*Another school,* she says, meaning, *Another county.* Close, but far enough for different.) "And, I don't know," my sister says, "she's just *not very nice.*" The haze of dust kicks up and presses on the windshield. "At parties," I say. A statement like a question. And she smirks. "At parties," she says. (And I wonder how it is I don't know more about her life. Or how it is her life became so separate from mine. I realize, too, that she doesn't know me either, or not so much now, anymore.) My sister speeds around a bend. Her headlights flash the yellow caution sign. We straighten out until the nothing's back before us, and the DJ on the radio speaks low and out of hearing. I don't know where my sister's going. (I'm not familiar with *out here*.) But soon, she's turning left onto another, shorter road. I finger the pack of cigarettes in my lap. I pick at its plastic wrap. Up ahead, a window the color of rust hovers above the earth. It's our mother and her husband's house, and our mother's left a light on. Beside the house, a large garage sits almost lonely in the dark. Its door shades something blue from the white glow far above it. The moon, and full tonight. The car crawls up and tints the blue to white to yellow, and the headlights on the big door's surface focus into orbs. We sit quiet. Engine running. Small flying bugs flick shadows on the wall like black confetti. "Thanks," I say. (For driving.) I pull the wrapper off the carton in my lap. Crumple it together to a loose ball in my hand. My sister takes the wrapper off of me and shoves it, rough, into the cupholder. "So," she says, and looking at the carton in my grip. "When did *that* start?" she asks. "It didn't start," I say, and "Well," and then, "Not *really*, anyway." I tell her that a boy I think I love tries smoke rings in the dark. That he has hands that smell, sometimes, like them. That most nights now, I say, I lean against the railing of his balcony. (And when he sucks at cigarettes, he makes a sort of kissing sound. Like it's the most natural thing in the world. And smoke curls up from lips that let it—*vanishes*—past red cheeks like kettle heat to start again. It goes on rising from his hand.) "I don't *really* smoke," I say. (I just think I'm trying to.) "It's stupid," and I laugh. (It is, I think—but I don't say—*so that I might have something out here.*) She tells me that she doesn't care, who gives a fuck. But when I ask her if she wants one, she just shakes her head. "I'm good." She turns her car off, and there's the jingle of her keys. And there's the engine, dying. And everything goes quiet. Goes dark. (For a moment.) Until the world appears in phases: the driveway's pavement—the grass—the empty space around the house. All shaded silver from the moon. I push the car's door open, and I step onto the gravel. It's hard under my feet and has a sound like biting down. I tell my sister that I want to sit outside. Just a moment, long enough to settle on the pavement. Long enough to smoke, I tell her, one or two. Why not. And she tells me that she's cold. Her shoulders lift, her body shakes. (She's loud about it.) "I'll be inside," she says, and smiles, and soon it's only me. A couple crickets. The wind like rain in the mesquite. I fish the lighter from my pocket and wonder what it is about this life that draws our mother to it. This house that's far from anything. This man. I pull a cigarette out from the pack and set it between my lips. I spark the flame to light it and inhale. A weight presses to my chest—and lifts. And I'm lightheaded, just a moment. Just enough. I look down at the glowing ring around the cigarette's end and hope my sister gets away from here. From this place that's not our home but theirs. And our mother tries, I think, but in this house, she stretches blinds across the windows so the daylight can't push through. She neglects to decorate the walls so that the hallways remain bare. She runs water at the sink, and holds her hands under the water, and she stares at all the water flowing down the drain. The suds that pop, that spin. That disappear. Her husband, he reclines and turns the TV up until it's blaring so that the room is filled with nothing but the sound of it. He

stands out in the front yard with a rifle to the sky and follows birds,
and birds fall. He races fast cars on the backroads with his sons. I
shake and lift the cigarette. The orange glow. The chest weight and
the lift. I feel my body rocking something careful like the bowing
of the tall grass in the front yard. I tap the nail of my thumb against
the cigarette and watch it cough up hanging ash. Watch the ash
crash, scatter on the white rock near my shoe. Near the edge of
pavement, where I bend down into a sit. His sons, I think. Three
sons. (Three brothers.) They rev the engines of their Mustangs to
collective roars. They speed the open roads and slam on brakes and
drift. They conjure great white clouds of dust that eat the space
around them. Smoke eats the space around my head until it
doesn't. And I've never been too good with other men. At talking.
At connecting. The night before my mother's wedding, I sat inside
my car and watched the time outside the house they'd rented. I
considered driving off. The center console of the dashboard cast a
blue-green hue that gave the car's interior a look like it was sinking,
or that it'd already sunk. I stared at the house with the radio shut
off to calm my nerves. Nothing but the sound of the A/C and my
own breathing. (A deep inhale—a loud exhale. My therapist says
to think of thoughts like leaves on running water. Like clouds in
the sky. They may clutter to a mess, he says. They may grow dark
and fat with storm. But hold out. A deep inhale—a loud exhale—
and watch them pass.) The night before my mother's wedding, I
watched the front door of the house crack open, open slow. I
watched the dark shape of a man take up its center. Lift a hand.
We'd met before, but only once. At a restaurant in Denton, Texas,
where we'd had our first conversation at a corner table draped in
smooth white cloth. With a candle and a basket of bread at its center. (I can't remember what we'd talked about, but the food was

just okay. I'd tried and failed to keep my eyes off of my mother's new engagement ring.) And there came a sudden tapping on my window, and I jumped. My sister stood outside the car and waved. I shut the engine off, and still, the console held its glowing. Short inhale, short exhale. When she opened up the door, the blue-green shifted suddenly to black. "You good?" she asked. I nodded. "They all wanted to come outside," she said. And I felt the outside rushing in. A chill. (Three brothers.) "To meet you at your car." I stepped out onto the street and hugged her. "I told them that it might be overwhelming for you, though," she said. A low thing in my ear. "Meeting them for the first time and all, like this." And as we pulled apart, he walked right up. The man our mother would marry in the morning. Taller than our father by just a bit. With hair so blonde it's white. "They're excited to meet you," he said. I lied and told him that I felt the same. That it was good to see him again. (For the second time. The night before my mother's wedding.) He might've hugged me then. He might've shaken my hand. But together with my sister, this man led me to the front door of the house. Where, through the window on the front porch, I heard the sound of laughter on its other side. And, through the open doorway, I saw my mother seeing me among a family of strangers. I lift the cigarette and inhale, hold it, and exhale. I rub the bottom of my shoe against a clump of ash that's settled on the pavement. It smears a wave like charcoal on the cool gray surface, and I wonder if he'll see it in the morning. If my mother will. And on the morning of my mother's wedding, I wasn't sure what to do with myself. Where to go. I dressed myself. Carved silent trails through the bedroom to the bathroom to the kitchen of the rental house. I avoided conversation where I could. If I could. (I smiled where I couldn't.) I passed a doorway opened to a crack, and through the crack, I saw my mother. Inside and alone. Standing in front of a tall mirror and looking ahead at herself. Her dark hair had been pulled back to fall between her shoulders. Her dress looked close to cream and leveled at her chest. She wore pearls on her ears, around her neck. And at her sides, her hands, polished, manicured, rubbed nervous at themselves. They stilled—and her reflection pressed both hands together, overlapped, and light, against her heart. I knocked. My mother turned around. She smiled. I stepped inside and moved the door back to its crack. "You look really beautiful," I said. (I meant it.) My mother looked down at herself. Back to me. "Thank you, baby." And then I asked her how she felt. She turned back to her reflection in the mirror, smoothed the fabric at her stomach. "Nervous," she said. "Happy," she smiled. She forced a smile. Behind her, to the bedroom's balcony and the backyard just below it, the world looked drained of its color. The sky had blanketed itself in gray. The surface of the squarish pool in the backyard's center rocked and lifted minor waves. And I waited for my mother to ask me how I felt. (I wondered then if, maybe, she couldn't see me. Not really. Or, if she could—and I suspected that she might—she didn't have the heart, then, to address it. Not on the morning of her wedding.) And the light wood of the balcony outside grew sudden dark and scattered spots. And the water in the pool grew pockmarked with the rainfall. "I was afraid of that," my mother said. We both stood staring at the droplets forming on the window, racing down, collecting. And my mother's friend pushed through the door, holding a bouquet. Purple flowers. Pink. She apologized for barging in, but I just brushed it off. No worries. "Well," I said, about the rain, "they call it luck, I guess." And the reflection of my mother turned to face me as I slipped back to the hallway. Where the sound of everything outside beat rhythms in the quiet. Now, at my mother and her husband's house, the wind has died to quiet, and the tops of the mesquite hold still. And the crickets aren't disturbed enough to sing. The cigarette's a stub, burned down so that it's almost out. Its ring of orange is dying. I press it, dig it into rock. I twist my wrist and watch the movement snuff the color out. From where I sit on top the edge of pavement, I set what's left of the cigarette on the ashy streak and pull my legs into my chest and feel my heart, its beating hard against myself. I lean into it. And I remember how it seemed we'd never find the church that day. The small white chapel. How it felt hidden in a maze's end of elm and oak, and on and on down roads I'd never been. And the rain slowed as we got there. As we went inside and waited. As the planners prepped the speakers and the preacher and the *where-you're-supposed-to-gos.* I stood with my sister at the front door of the church with an arm linked through our mother's. The music, like a signal, sparked alive and crackled with the wireless speakers. Wrong song, or else it must've been because it changed mid-lyric. And just before the walk, I looked down to the aisle. To my feet. Down from that stranger and his family. Down from that new man. A father. Three brothers at the chapel's other end. (And I thought about our father. And I wondered where he might be. And I wondered if he knew that this was happening.) "What's wrong?" my mother asked. Hushed. For the three of us standing at the entrance. "What's wrong?" And I shook my head. (And this song that's playing, I thought, it must be their song. And this chapel, I thought, this town, it's their community.) "Just don't talk," my sister said, to our mother. To our mother: go. And the small crowd stood from pews and turned to see us walk between them. And the sun beamed through the windows. And here, the moon shines bright against the windshield of my sister's car and mine beside it. There's a rustling noise somewhere among the trees that line the property. It's too dark to see what ambles through them, but its noise is presence enough. I grab the cigarette, grip it with my fingers. I press my palms against the pavement, and I push to stand. I brush the backside of my jeans.

I inhale, deep—I exhale, loud.

Loud enough to hear the nearby rustling start again. To see my breath like smoke float up ahead of me, expel and leave me. Blend into the night. I walk the cigarette to the trashcan.

I hurry, step inside.

CHILD OF THE CLOUDED BROW

We are but older children, dear, / Who fret . . .
—Lewis Carroll, "Child of the
Pure Unclouded Brow"

The world outside holds gray: the neighborhood's all cold and still against the shadow of itself. The street's a mix of bright pale whites and Rudolph reds so that each house appears enflamed with color. Every driveway's muddied with it, those blended shades, and it's quiet on the street where all the houses look the same: drenched in a light that turns the sky rust-orange. Where every other house bears an illuminated cross in the front yard, a nativity set. Small, dirtied baby dolls in straw-stuffed mangers. It's been so long since he's been back. This son. His family's home again for Christmas, he thinks, and still—they're scattered. He stands outside his car and breathes it in, feels that cold expansion of the chest, that quiet letting go. It makes him anxious, home: West Texas, where here—on this unfamiliar street—he turns to see his mother's car. It's parked inside the driveway of the house with wilting yellow pansies out front. Not her house, but C's: her best friend, the one she's here to visit. He sniffs the air. He rubs his nose. Walks up the drive and breathes: cold expansion, letting go.

Again, until anxiety subsides, he breathes.

He'd never seen C's house, though he'd heard of it before. His mother, she'd invited him to see it. Curious, he thinks, to have a place so *known*. From an outside view, the house looks so much like its neighbors: a weather-beaten slated roof leans out to grasp the wooden posts that hold it up, the porch; terracotta tiles, like slots of honeycomb, lead up and to the doorway, past the white painted cut-out of a rabbit running toward it; and the Christmas lights look nothing like the ones across the street: they shine dull in comparison, he thinks. There's nothing special about this place, and so he wonders why he's here. He looks down and to his wrist. The lights appear as yellow orbs in the watch's face from above until he shifts his wrist to see the hands, aimed up and to the left. Approaching midnight. He's late, he thinks, but then—his mother says—C never sleeps. And then he's at the door, and he's reflected in the glass: that glass door that guards the other, solid one behind it. He's lit from behind with all the lights along the roof and the ones across the street, and so his reflection looks back dark. Featureless. As if in half-melt, and the glass itself shines with a bright and silver mist. When he rings the doorbell, he hears a quiet shuffling on the other side. Distant. And laughter, moving close. He stands alone to wonder about what might happen next until the front door opens, suddenly—the solid one—and it's his mother, standing there behind the glass. She smiles as she turns the handle, pushes—*Hey, baby*—and hugs him tight. Pulls

him

in.

And they're everywhere: hands, sprouting like some alien crop
from the mantel and the bookshelves and the tables in the
living room—each reaching up and holding out for nothing.

They live in forms of black plastic. Of porcelain. Of a cool, dull
metal like copper, or Styrofoam coated in a thick silver spray
paint. They throw peace signs and "OK" and "I love you" in
sign language. They shake a surfer's "hang loose." Palm-forward,
embedded in concrete, one hand looks like anticipation.
For touch, maybe. Or a way out of itself. A purple *hamsa* eyes
him, hanging low from the living room ceiling. Another,
behind a chair. Another, behind the row of fish tanks.

And he'd never seen his mother like this before:
cross-legged, sitting up, and wearing smoke as a veil. The air smells
like a forest, he thinks, and his mother laughs. Coughs rough
and laughs, because it's funny. Passes on the pipe. He notices his
mother's always smiling at what's said, and when she does, she
tucks dark strands of hair up and over, behind her left ear, her
right, before both hands settle at her lap. She looks almost child-
like, he thinks. Giddy. With every puff of smoke, she pushes back
against the old mother, the one from childhood: that woman
based in Proverbs, concerned with healthy living. Her eyes spark
when laughter boils up and out, and they begin to squint. As
if too much light is precious. As if it must be kept inside, pre-
served somehow. He notices those eyes are red, bright red. That
all their eyes, he thinks, are *red,* and C sits laughing among the
pillows of her bed. She's short and stout to his mother's tall and
lean, and she's prone to joking at her size. Her hands are quick
to pile green into another bowl, and when she does—looks
down to pinch what's in the silver grinder—small layers of thick
fat cushion up against her chin. Her lips purse in contempla-
tion, as if the loading of the bowl is something philosophical.
It's really something, he says, about her home, and she throws

her arms into the air, that loaded pipe in-hand. *Welcome to my mind.* They are a trio getting high and sinking down into C's bed:
down a rabbit hole, he thinks, and
he
shakes
it
off.

Anxiety rises:
he breathes in,
lets it go.

The lower halves of painted faces give features to the walls. One's framed in black with big lips grinning in a muted shade like blood-rush. Another half-face sits below the painting of a ballgown and holds atop itself a pair of high heels and flowers, a Grecian bust and a portrait of a bullfrog—all sitting grouped together on the tabletop that cuts right through the face's nose. Beside a black leather chair, a second decapitated head. An antique lamp sits where the face's eyes should be, and beneath the coverage of the metal lampshade, a pile of them: eyes, each one glass and painted with a stare. Each looking at something in the rooms they can never put a word to.

Longing: the whole house, full of it.

Fuck 'em all, right? C takes the pipe and blocks its airflow. She's sucking in, deep. She watches as the bowl flickers orange and glows, and she holds it there, like that. Then lets it all go. *Fuck all them fucking fuckers,* C says through thick smoke. She laughs in the haze and then repeats this process. And when she laughs, it sounds like joy, and she's contagious: C, with black hair cut short so that it spikes. With thin lips always grinning big in red. The smoke lets out from nostrils, those pursed lips, and lifts. It disperses almost as it joins together, and a shade of blue hovers in the air around them. This is her house, her bedroom, he thinks. She can say whatever the fuck she wants. And when C talks about work, his mother laughs the hardest. They vent about the men there, the self-righteous ones in sea-green scrubs and white coats they used to work for—not so long ago, together. *Those cocksuckers,* C says as she passes the pipe. He watches his mother take it with something nearing caution. She holds it for a bit before she turns to C and says, *You'll have to light it.* C shakes her head. Rolls her eyes. She looks right at him and points, to his mother. *Do you see this?* she asks. She makes a ticking sound with her mouth. She laughs—they all do—as C leans forward with the lighter, and the bowl catches the flame. His mother inhales and holds it—holds it—too long, and she coughs it up. Waves away the smoke that all comes rushing through a smile. C makes that ticking sound. *Jesus, woman.* She pats her best friend hard on the back. *Just like a child.* And she turns to him, and she winks. He learns a term then: *Bogarting.* After the famous actor's known habit of holding on to any unlit cigarette. Of letting them hold balance in the corner of his mouth. Not drawing in, so never letting out. C says, *You're bogarting it.* "It," here, being the pipe. The one that's on its third or fourth round around the circle now. She says, *Teach it to your friends.* C blows thick rings to the ceiling. She seems to run on smoke, and the glow of the bedroom's single fish tank drowns them all in turquoise. His mother's hue, he thinks, her favorite color. And when the pipe comes to her, she passes it immediately.

Or else, she doesn't touch it. She isn't smoking anymore, so she lets her son go on. Take it.   Bogart it. Once they've put the pipe aside to rest, C turns to the bookshelf beside the bed. These books, she says, she takes and blacks them out. Makes poetry, draws portraits. She keeps them on a shelf for when she has friends over, and his mother nods at this. Smiles. He can't stop thinking about his mother's age: how young she looks right now, and still—how tired. *I've done it for a long time,* C says. *With old books like this.* Collective art, she calls it. And when she pulls a few and drops them on the bed, there's the quick pressure-sound of the bedsprings pushing back. *Pick a book,* she says. There's a worn Bible, a Quran; a large, collected Nietzsche, and a tattered-looking dictionary. He wonders which one has his mother's words inside, her sketchings. He tries to picture what she'd mark in Psalms—if it's the Bible that she'd chosen some time ago. Or Proverbs: that Proverbs woman. But he can't seem to hold the image, and he points at the dictionary. Its leather cover's almost torn, and the words, he sees, have long-since faded into yellow. She hands him the book and tells him, *Pick a page.* He flips through pages colored in the margins and lands on one that's empty: black and white. And when he does, she passes on a box of crayons, top flipped open. Their heads stick out just barely from that snug place. They look almost sleeplike, he thinks, the crayons— like they're sleeping. And C says, *Pick a color.* He stares a while to be sure. He pulls it out: a deep red. Like so many of the house's lips. It must be why he chose it, he thinks, and he runs a fingertip across the color. Against that soft wax. He wonders if everyone does this just before they start. A habit, he thinks—he knows— that he must have formed in childhood. He guides an open palm across the page. *It's yours,* C says. *Now, what is it you want to say?*

He breathes in.   Holds it.   Lets it go.
And the absurdity's not lost on him: the fact that it's his mother—
this strange, new mother—and his mother's stoner friend: late-
forty-somethings getting high and talking life with one who feels
as if he's just beginning. Or, who sometimes feels life's at its end.
He doesn't say this out-loud, because he knows it all sounds crazy:
calling this, just 24, the end. That there's so much more beyond this
place, this town, the people that he knows. His wayward family.
He wonders, for a moment, how it was exactly that they got here.
To this house, this bed, with this screen of smoke around them.
As his mother speaks to C, he presses one palm into the other. He
smiles so that he's present. So that he doesn't show his thinking. He
reaches for his water when this thinking overwhelms him, and in
his state, the thoughts, they come in flashes: he can't help but see
the mother who was once so afraid of drugs. Who cried whenever
she believed her son had turned away from God. This is not my
mother now, he thinks. She's gone and left me here. But then he
knows this isn't true, not really. And he turns onto another thought:
the truth, he thinks, is that his world feels larger now, and, somehow, in its growing, *empty.* He wonders if all the adult children
of divorce feel this way. If home, or the idea of home, had only
seemed to mean something in the *after.* But then, how can one ever
really know when something's good? When it's *right?* His mother,
drawing on her stacks of self-help books and talks and classes, calls
it a *gut feeling.* As if choice is all intuitive. In parked cars or in living rooms, whenever they're alone these days, she looks at him with
sad eyes—her own made choices hide, he thinks, behind so much
broken green. And she says, *You just know when you know.* She taps
her chest, the place above her heart. Where he once believed some
Spirit to be. *You just have to believe it's right,* she says, and, *Trust*

God's plan. He wants to roll his eyes at this—but he holds back. No, his mother's not completely gone, he thinks. Just finding her own way mid-way through life. He knows that all he wants is to be told exactly what to do, and this thought troubles him. How, he wonders, are we ever meant to find a way back out? He rubs his palms. How do we make it back home, to where we want to be? And then, from far-off,

a lone train's whistle slices through his trailing thoughts and brings him back to now. He thinks the trains sound different where he's from. This one roars from not-so-far-away, and when it does, he pauses. The *where he's from* is *here,* he thinks. It all comes back to home. He looks to this new mother. Suddenly, grows anxious. Runs fingers through his hair and looks back down to that hollowed space inside his circle of crossed legs. He feels like he's a kid again. Like something's wrong—*this*—but no one's saying anything. And things are always changing. Maybe, he thinks, he's lost control of what can change. So it's a reflex, when he grins. As they all erupt in laughter. As he sees the wall behind the bed grinning too:
a painted face, grinning forward,
with lips that seek to
swallow him
alive.

He takes a drink of water.
He holds it in his mouth
until it loses all its cool.
Swallows.

Breathes.

His mother's laughter's sparked from C, who sits among piled pillows when she tells her tales. Like a middle-aged and stoned Scheherazade, he thinks, and he loves how she looks. How tall she sits. He thinks they must look so small next to her, when she pats her knees. Grips them. C talks about the sixteen-year-old cat approaching seventeen, and when she does, they look to see him creep beneath the bedroom's fish tank: he's here, her story's shadow. And the cat's body's small and gray and thin, and slow— his creep's a labor. His mother shakes her head. He knows that cats have never been *her thing*—she's allergic, so of course. Her shake reads disapproval, but in a loving way. And she smiles. She's always smiling around people. C tells of how this cat had killed a bird the other day. How he brought it in and set it in the doorway. And the punchline, as if fragility weren't enough: *He's declawed.*

His mother laughs at this, what seems impossible.

He laughs—he thinks—to ward away the walls:
walls glossed with metal keys and chains of silver beads
and tearoom candles. They hold in-place, enshrined in empty
picture frames. It's so unlike the walls of childhood, his
mother's walls—those white walls covered in her crosses.
Thick panes of tall stained-glass float behind the enormous
living room window where he imagines, in the daytime,
the sun must filter through in scattered rays of blue
and green and purple. And hanging up, beside the
painted fireplace: the portrait of a woman, gazing
off—away—that C had painted over. *I didn't like
the color of her dress,* she says, and so she'd made it red.
The floor's an old light wood, and there's a barely
sunken section in the middle. It had once been carpet—

C says, about the sunken place—that she'd ripped up,
painted over. The result of almost everything's all C's
imagination: her home, a recreation. The floor's
a sky-blue backdrop with black-and-white fanned
feathered shapes that curl like waves. And there,
he sees a bright red flower—it flares beneath the couch.
Above their heads and lining every doorway, entryway,
the length of that big window: wreathes of tulle, each
with a theme. One's all white, with Christmas balls and
pearls and snowflakes; one's all red and white and blue,
with giant stars inside its center; one's all turquoise,
holding shells and small pink starfish. He's reminded
C can't sleep—that that's why she creates. Two fish
tanks hug the wall. They provide the music for the room:
that low buzz-hum, those constant bubbles. One houses two
big turtles, and the other, neon fish. C says she'd had to
separate a few, a night or two ago—that she had to move
some fish from one tank to the other. *Those fuckers,* she says,
they always thought they had to fight. She taps the glass.
It sounds so hollow, he thinks, and C, she shakes her head.
C leads them underneath a leopard-spotted wreath and down
the hallway. She steps with the slightest limp, but her walking
speed is quick. *On my feet all day,* he knows she'd say, and might
laugh about getting older. His mother trails not far behind her.
He keeps up the rear. He feels as if he's pulled along, has been
this whole time. Like he's floating in his highness, or else still
sinking lower. And his mother: she walks, amazed. She's seen it
all before, he thinks, and still, she's quick to ask for stories.
She's hungry for the origins of things inside C's home.

It's a history he thinks, his mother seems to admire—

C's   endless   pool   of   lived   experience.

C stops. Turns, and gestures to an open doorway at her right:
My mother-in-law stays here, C says, *whenever she's around. But she's
always on the road.* He watches as C's big red eyes grow bigger. She
leans into a whisper: *And thank* God *for the road.* She flips the light
switch on, and the room is steeped in purple: from the bedspread
to the curtains to the vanity against the wall, and C shrugs. *She
likes purple,* and she turns the color back to black.

At the end of the hall, they take a left
into the only room this far down—the house's depths. He feels
his smile stretch, and he can't help it: stuffed bears line the upper
shelves that wrap around the room. They sit tall in rocking chairs,
or else they're gathered on the floor. The bed is full of bears where,
in another house, he thinks, throw pillows might stack up. *My collection,* she says. One of many, he thinks, and to him, it feels familiar—all these stuffed bears. He watches as his mother thumbs the
bright red ribbon of a bear that's sitting on the dresser. *Oh,* and
then she turns to him. *He looks like Curly Bear,* she says. Like childhood. His mother's tone is warm, and still—her shoulders tense up
where she stands. Her hands,

they wring themselves. And there
are pictures of C's family on the dresser: her son, she says, a boy
around his age—23 or 24, though here, he's mostly just a child.
In one, he stands below his mother; she wraps behind him at the
shoulders. His smile's small, hardly there. His nose and chin are

sharp. His hair is blond, pushed to the side. They look nothing like family, he thinks, and wonders what this thinking means. *My little dealer,* C says, and laughs. Shakes her head. Makes that ticking with her mouth.

He remembers to breathe
when C gestures to a large doll's table nearby, arranged on a low shelf. The company's familiar: an innocent-looking Alice sits across from a lightly fluffed March Hare; an orange-haired Mad Hatter looms pale and serious at the table's head; and three small and unrelated bears sit in their own places along the stretch of table. He'd heard about her love for Wonderland—his mother had told him once about the growing tattoo on C's back. In fact, he'd seen it, sometime years before. His mother had shown him a picture, the one that C had sent: of C's bare back, exposed— the camera flash, so bright against pale skin. He thinks about it now—and all at once, he finds himself drifting, lost in thinking: in thin and twisted silver smoke floating just below C's shoulder: *WHO ARE YOU?* The question drifts out from the plump blue caterpillar smoking on a big red-spotted mushroom: and at the mushroom's base, a tree line: a dirt path that leads into a purple wood, to clustered wooden signposts: each points their different courses, and he pauses: he takes the one that *feels right*: (he hears his mother's voice): a path to butterflies of bread that flap along C's back: they rise from white and form into a Cheshire grin: it says something about madness, all this, he thinks, and then his path gets bright: it opens up into an orchard, to giant roses hanging in the trees: some are white and some are
dripping:
dripping:
dripping a delicious candy-red: and all the cards hold brushes, and

on those brushes, red: the Queen of Hearts, her dress her hair her
angry face is: red,

               and then he's suddenly pulled down, pulled
back, inside the room of bears. His mother stands with both arms
crossed and bites her fingernails. *I saw you looking,* C says to him
and smiles. She points behind the tea party. He'd been staring off
and looking toward the dark and shrunken thing there, at the feet
of Alice. He'd thought it looked a little odd. Drained of color: a
sick tan bordering black. C picks it up. She sets it in his hand,
and he turns it. Rubs a thumb against it. He finds it hard, like
textured leather. *Put a lemon in a room?* she says. *It drains the negativity. Holds it in and starts to look like this.* She taps what's in
his palm. And then he starts to notice, as they move around the
house: beside a fish tank; in a hand that's sitting on the mantel;
on cookbooks, nightstands, in the painted wicker baskets above
the bathrooms' toilets—lemons, everywhere. Like the house's
scattered body parts. What a concept, he thinks: all those lemons, full of captured negativity. His mother palms one, holds
it up. *I'll try it, when I get back home.* He knows he'll try it too.

He notices, in passing, the boxy Polaroid on the fridge: of
a man—about C's age—in an orange prison jumpsuit. His
dark plastic glasses glare in bold fluorescent light. His hair
is blond, buzzed. He smiles small, and C stands smiling
big beside him. The thin gold rings on their left hands, he
thinks, tell more than both their smiles. *25 years,* he remembers his mother saying. And he remembers how his mother
shook her head when she talked about it. Closed her eyes
and crossed her arms. She can't imagine it, that time. But
here, he thinks C's eyes read sad, and still—there's hope.

He feels the night is coming to an end. That their high is running out, and he still can't seem to shake it: his mother's absence. How, in the moments she comes through, it's in her laughter. When she claps, can't catch her breath. When she says C's name. *You're crazy,* his mother says to her. She squeezes both eyes shut and rocks back, forward, as she buckles to her laughter on the bed. Just like he sometimes does. *You're so crazy,* she says to C—the freedom that his mother wants. The force she feels she needs to lean on in order to get by. The strength. Yes, he thinks, there's an independence to this place his mother seems to crave. C has crafted her own world. She's *made* her independence. And still, his mother told him that C hardly ever leaves it. That she's too anxious outside of it. Beyond the rooms, he thinks, that are her own. He pictures C here, alone, and wonders what it is his mother seeks to find. He breathes in just enough to break the feeling up,   enough to *hide* his feelings, and he listens to his mother. When the room's eyes are on her, she does impressions of the people she and C used to know. Of memorable patients, like one of her old favorites: the elderly man who'd been known to shuffle both feet forward, down the hallway in his wheelchair. Who must've had a stroke some time just before they'd met—who'd always called her *sweetheart,* smiled back. He remembers when the old man passed, and how his mother cried at dinner. How she wrung her hands in feeling at his absence. *Slow progress is progress,* C says about their old friend's wheelchair shuffle, making light of their sad world. And his mother smiles. Nods. *Yes,* she says, and to whatever: *Yes.* It's the agreement he's afraid of—that he sometimes sees rising up in himself. He thinks she's never who she wants to be, not yet, and so she molds. Smiles to smile. Laughs to laugh. Because when the room's eyes are not on her, the son sees someone different. Someone more like himself: a smirk that melts into worry. A bitten bottom lip. A closed mouth that moves in subtle shifts, first right then left—she bites her inner cheeks. And when she's lost in thought, her eyes go to her hands. Her eyes are always on her hands, he thinks, and her hands: they reach out for themselves. They hold themselves. Her thumbs, they take turns digging into palms. Kneading. And *needing*: something, whatever's on her mind. She's spent so much of life now, needing—and, he knows, she's finding her way back. From here: another divorce. From a man, so brief, after his father. *Another failure,* she says. But he and C, he knows, they see it for what it really is: her freedom. A chance, now, to run from molding into men that do not suit her; from feeling weak, unlike herself, beside those men. He thinks it's possible that she's become a victim to her needing, and that, maybe, she can't stop looking for some place to let it go. That what she fears is having so much left to hold on to. Or, that she's not where she wants to be.

(*How*—like him, his mother must think—*did we all get here?*)

And it's well past three when they head back out—no, up, he thinks, back *up* and from the depths: through all those rooms of severed hands

and lips in picture frames,

of eyes

and bears

and lemons.

In the turtle tank, one stretches out his neck on top the tank's large rock. The rock is like an island in the middle of the tank, and he

watches as the other turtle surfaces close-by. The swimmer climbs
up so that they're stranded there together,

and the water stills.

Soon, he's back outside. His mother walks him out. She's staying
here tonight and might not see him in the morning. Might not
see him for a while. She walks a bit ahead as he turns to hug C
bye. She holds him with a squeeze. *You take care of your mother,*
C says. And he nods. *She'll figure things out,* he says, and then he
realizes how this sounds: like maybe she should try and make it
on her own. *I mean,* he says, too quick, *I will.* And C nods back.
She hugs him tight, again. And when he meets his mother at his
car parked in the driveway, he turns to see the glass door, dark.
The house's solid door has closed. Now, he thinks, in all that
early morning gray, he sees his mother's face reflecting light: she
holds the porch's glow. The colors of the street. And the house,
he thinks, on leaving it, looks nothing like its center. *Pretty
wild, huh,* his mother says. Smiles. And it's a flash from younger
days: of singing ABBA in the car, and loud, with every window
down. She looks ahead. This early world, he thinks, is freezing.
He breathes it in.   Lets breathing go.
    They stand outside and watch as moths fly desperate into
windows.

IN CASE YOU FIND US UNRESPONSIVE

I've been thinking, Dad, about November. That day when I sat passenger, and your daughter, M, sat in the backseat, and you drove us in your truck from this, your parents' place in Post, Texas, out to our childhood family home. When just before we passed the house, you slowed us down to look. And there's nothing out there, still, except the property itself and the surrounding cotton fields, but we all could see the place has changed: trees have been stripped down to nothing now where, before, when the four of us had lived there as a family, there'd been so many of them; as a kid, I'd labeled it a forest, and it ran against the edge of that open cotton sea. That spotted brown and white and green. A wire fence now circles round the property so that the whole house looks constricted, and the bright red metal barn remains—the one whose roof had been ripped off, away, when we had lived there, tossed like nothing to land several miles from our home. Today, its roof appears intact.

(We'd all gone underground most times, but that storm felt different at the start: I remember how you woke me up, at 8 or 9 or 10, whatever year it was, and I started screaming from the noise, from the hail beating on the windows, and the close trees scratching at the glass, and the wind howling through the fireplace. I remember how you put me and my sister in your bedroom, on your bed, and you told me, *Wait*, to *Stay right there,* as you and then my mother ran into the living room. And because I feared that I would lose you both—I always feared your deaths—I told my sister, *Wait,* to *Stay right there,* and I followed the sounds of your yelling. Of my mother's screaming. And I watched her rush to save the carpet, and I watched you rush to save the windows: you stood outside the house and hammered wooden boards across the broken glass as hail beat hard against your back, and my mother screamed your name. She caught me standing in the doorway of that scene, barely, in the dark, and she screamed mine. But her voice was lost like all of ours. Muted, beneath it all. Back inside, you rushed your family to the car, and we drove through water rising on the road. You stopped to get a neighbor—a woman living down that road, alone—and the five of us fled—crawled—toward town. I stared outside my window to a nothing sight: and in several hurried flashes of light, I saw that mad tornado.)

Today, a horse corral and track that wasn't ours stands right behind that barn. And my fort—or, what I had called my *fort*: the giant bush standing sentry in the driveway that I'd once gutted over several days one summer; I'd started from the outer edge and worked my way inside it, digging to its center, tossing every little branch outside its new-formed entryway, and I'd spend long afternoons inside of it, hidden, in a world of my own, and I'd stare through shaded green at you, Dad, working underneath the shaded carport on the other side, or at my mother, gathering water for the garden with her metal bucket, or at my little sister, carrying in both her arms the newest litter of our old dog's puppies—that fort had lost its every layer of protection so that the inside can be seen completely, still hollowed-out. And now, the once great bush looks bare. And the house—

We stared for a while. M shook her head. I looked past you. You sniffed, bit at your lip.

The three of us drove on.

You told us then, as the house shrunk in the rearview, how, one day, you came out on your own and knocked. You told whoever opened up the door that you once lived here. That, years and years ago, it'd been your family's home. You told them how, over a summer, you'd tiled the master bathroom, and you'd painted all the walls, and, if it's okay, you said—if it's not too much to ask— you'd like to see the inside one last time. This new family let you in to walk the dining room, and the kitchen, and beneath the tall, beamed ceilings in the living room, snapping with your phone the pictures that you'd later show us. And I imagine how you pointed, how you told these people about us, your son and daughter, now 24, now 20. Not much had changed since we were little, you said—about the inside of the house. But then you told us that you never asked to see the bedrooms, where this new couple and their children sleep. This, you said, felt too invasive—so I couldn't ask you if the walls of where I used to sleep in childhood remain, still, painted blue.

(I don't tell you that I miss this life sometimes, but I confess: *I miss that blue.*)

On the way back into town, I splayed my hands along my thighs in silence. I rubbed my palms against rough denim, felt the sweat soak through. I looked over to my right and out the window—caught the unclear outline of the two of us reflected in the glass. You: with your brown Carhartt and the graying hair that

frames your mouth, the broken skin on hands that holds this country's dirt. Me: with my black jeans, my flannel overshirt—clean
clothes—and my bare face whose hair that grows, when it does, in
patches. We share the same eyes, or almost: they squint along with
laughter, and they look, most days, a step away from tears.

Your eyes: they'd hung, the whole way there and back, on the
mirror, on M, behind you.

Because you're terrified—it's clear—that you've lost her. (But
you don't see me watching you, watching her. Can't know that, in
my own way, I'm terrified I've lost you too.)

When the drive back into town put M to sleep, your attention
held, mostly, to the road. Now, to me. And I asked you how you
feel. When you come back out here, to the country. To West Texas.
Or home. I'd wanted to know, then, if you ever feel the same way
that I do: so bare and sad and vulnerable, so far-removed from a
life that doesn't feel like it's my own now anymore. And *sorry*, in a
way, or several ways. But you couldn't put your feelings into words.
I watched you try in silence, for nothing. And there's nothing out
the window too: faded earth and open sky. A world where everything, I think, seems central, now, to nowhere. Anyway, I told
you that you can't expect to feel the same on coming home when
you've gone away and changed, so much.

(I said it for the both of us.)

NOW, I know it sounds ridiculous. Trust me, Dad: I do. But sometimes, when I look back, I start to think about it: the letter that
I wish I could've written you that night. The letter that I would
have, if only I were able. When, just before the end, I might've
scratched a hurried mess into an empty spiral notebook. Of claus-

trophobic words that might've veered and crossed each page's every thin blue line. I might've left it somewhere close for you to find, that letter, full of all the things I'd never had the chance to tell you. Then and now. And all in case we really might've died.

But then, of course, I didn't. Write it, I mean. And then, of course, *we* didn't. Die.

So, this is it: we'll try again: just picture it's the end:

I'm sorry. That this is how things go. Have gone. That this is how you'll find me and M here in the morning: our bodies sprawled out on a pullout couch where, I imagine, by the time you read this, all our skin shades gray or blue. Where both our heads bend awkward, up, against the couch's cushioned backs, mouths hanging stuck, wide open, like we've just been pulled from water. Buried under blankets in the guesthouse of our grandparents' backyard. What's called in bolded letters, on a sign above the door: LOVE SHACK.

I can tell you—and here's some comfort—that we laughed when we first saw that sign. Something that we'd, somehow, never noticed. We shook our heads, and M said, *Fucking weird.* Because it is: it's not really where you want to spend the night if you don't have to with your sibling. But we had to, because, tonight, the other house—the real one, at our backs—is full of Thanksgiving. With your parents, and your girlfriend in another room, and you. And in the SHACK, there's just the couch's bed, a sink, a bathroom dimmed and tinted yellow by its overhead light; a TV that picks up only static; a closet full of quilts.

And well, Dad, now, there's us. Your children.

And I think we might be dying.

Let me explain:

When we first walked into the guesthouse, M tossed her bag

down on the pullout couch. Springs creaked, and at the sound, I'd looked up at the clock on the wall behind it. At its face: and its hands at minutes after midnight. M lifted up a Ziplock from the pocket of her backpack. Inside, a small tube made the plastic bag sway, and she opened it and reached inside—she freed the tube and twisted it; she pulled it, turned it over. And something slid out, into her open palm: a joint she'd saved for this. For us, and for reunion. We stepped out on the LOVE SHACK's porch and sat and watched a single light shine through a window on the backside of the house.

Look:

Outside, M sits down on a bench against the LOVE SHACK's wall and kicks her feet up on the porch's railing. She covers herself with a blanket, and I sit beside her, do the same. She pulls a lighter out from the inside pocket of her jacket and lifts the joint to put between her lips. She lets it dangle in the air and cups a hand around its end and strikes the lighter, and her face, for a moment, lights up orange. Her pale blue eyes trend gray. She's beautiful, I think, like our mother. (And then, I think: I know that you must see our mother in her too.) When the features of her face return to dark, there's just the color of the joint's end—a glow before it dies, slowly, back to black. I hear her hold the smoke in; I hear it flow out through a gap between her lips. And there's a feeling like shock that I can't shake, watching my younger sister—a child, still, to me sometimes—lighting up and getting high. But then she's holding out the joint to me, between two fingers of her left hand. She crosses her legs and leans forward, her right arm draped tight against her stomach like she's almost pained. Looking not at me but the exchange.

I take the smoking thing from her, and I put it to my mouth. I

don't need to light it, because it burns already: low, but it burns—
and it rises to that glow, and holds, and dies, again, when I pull it
away. The taste, I think, is strangely bitter, and it lingers, tingles on
my tongue. I hold the smoke in until it fills my chest, and I release.
I watch the smoke, by the light of the house's window, drift away
from us. And I worry—honestly, I do—that someone nearby or
inside might smell it, strong. I stare at the backdoor. I swim inside
my head. My leg begins to shake.

Cold? M asks.

I laugh. Yes, I say.

The truth is that I can't believe we're doing this, together, and
in our grandparents' backyard. Our grandparents: conservative,
Church of Christ regulars; the heads of our big family; *known* in
our old hometown of 5,000, up and down the street by neighbors,
with near-daily run-ins at the grocery store, the Pizza Hut, the
bank. Our grandad, now "retired," just won Farmer of the Year; our
grandma keeps a fat and growing rolodex of names and numbers in
the kitchen by the phone.

I ignore the paranoia. Or I attempt. I say, So, and let the word
hang as I turn to M.

How's it been? I ask. (Being around *you* again, is what I mean.)

It's a conversation, I realize, that we have, now, every time I see
her. When I see her.

M looks ahead. At the window. The joint's back in her hand,
between her lips, and she's letting out smoke. *I don't know,* she says.
It's weird. Back to me, and so's the joint. And it's her usual response
to asking how she is: *Things are weird.*

She doesn't want to let it go, I think, and I understand: that
Mexican restaurant parking lot just keeps on coming back. When
she called our mother's boyfriend *Dad* in front of you (her mistake,

I think, though another truth is that M can be, in her own way, intentionally malicious—she's always known, we know, how to hit a nerve), and you slapped her, hard, across the face (*your* mistake, and most likely, as she tells it, a drunk one). Still, my being far removed from it, I wonder at the pop, and if it echoed off, clapped against, the asphalt; I wonder at a witness in another car or on the sidewalk just outside the restaurant; I wonder at how quickly she cried, or if you did, and when.

Of course—you've always denied this event when pressed, and that's how our family seems to operate: we all have our own version of the same story, and it's near-contest that we tell it *right*.

He's never said he's sorry, she says, as new smokes drifts on over from my side.

He is, though, I say. He just—and I pass the joint—doesn't know how to talk.

M laughs. She's well aware.

(There's a family joke: and the punch line's about us Mason boys not knowing how to talk.)

Well, I say. I know he's happy that you came.

There's the sound, far-off, but near enough, of a neighbor's windchimes. Tires on gravel.

What about you? M asks.

What about me?

We both pause—freeze—at a shadow that speeds across the window and its light. A moth.

You and Dad.

We both stare at the window. M holds the joint in her fingers, but it hovers, near her lap.

He talks to me, I say. But—and I look up at the tree in the center of the yard, whose branches match the dark. About Mom, I say.

That's it?

I bite my lip. Feel my head nodding, a motion that doesn't seem to want to cease.

That's it.

Another moth, and another. They beat against the glass.

Have you talked to her? I ask. (Our mother.)

No, she shakes her head. *I mean,* she says, *not lately.* Smoke rises—and, *You?*

Sometimes, but—and I look down at my feet, near gone in the half-light. No, I say, not really.

It's been a few years now, since divorce. For a while there, our mother had been living in the new place with the new family: her high school sweetheart and his three sons. One lived at home, but the other two—our age—would visit often. I never really knew them. M, one day, having finally had enough, left our mother behind for an apartment of her own. And to our mother, it seemed M *ran away.* She felt, in some way, abandoned. (The truth, I think, is that our mother—now at the end of divorce from this new man, the man she thought her sweetheart—misses a life before our family's split. One day, in a new and empty townhome with just her mattress on the floor, a single lamp glowing dim beside it, she tells me that she's *sorry.* And she tells me that she misses you.)

Anyway, M says that she's much happier now. Being away from it all.

And as for me, I'd left for school before it all went south—and M became my witness.

Can you fucking believe *it?* M asks. *It's so* fucked, she says, and laughs. *So much has changed.*

And she's right. There's so much we don't touch; so much I don't say. Like how I came in through the backdoor one day, on what I'd later realize would be my last weekend going home, and you stood arched over the sink, alone in your silence and looking down and into it. Like how, that same weekend—an Easter weekend—at lunch, you reached to hold our mother's hand before she pulled away and off the table, covered up her chin, and kept on talking to the person at her right while you filled your mouth with what you had left over on your plate. Like how M led me into our bathroom back at home and shut the door, confirmed what I'd suspected in a whisper: *separation,* Mom's seeking-out divorce, and how I cried—the last to know—while M wrapped arms around me.

I felt angry—and I feel angry, still—that a family could be so quiet about something so *loud.*

It's hard, M says, *to keep up.*

She offers me the last of the joint, and I accept. Ash falls down from its end and lands in silent clumps—broken piles at our feet— and I stub out what's left of what we've shared against the bottom of my shoe.

IT'S SOMETHING you don't know, and now you do: that your children, much like you, share a fondness for the things that keep us lifted up and hold us there, outside of ourselves. A fancy way to say, I guess, that, *unlike* you, we smoke and—these days—smoke a lot. A *lot* a lot.

So, then, trust me when I say: *I know there's something very wrong here.*

We're sitting on that porch when I start to notice it. It's when M stares off, like she's prone to doing—when her eyes grow large and blink a couple times, and fast, to narrow down her gaze; when she wets her bottom lip and bites down quick behind her mouth. (And here she looks like our mother again: in how the effort of her thinking reads clear on her face; and she lifts dark strands of straightened hair, first over one and then the other ear.) M holds her stare onto the light that's on behind the murky window where our grandparents' bathroom sits inside the house. It's what we've both continued watching. The moths. We wait for something else that might eclipse the light, and soon: the thin shadow of a woman on the other side, maybe, or the outline of her nightgown. We sit silent in our smoke. What's left of it, at least: a dull haze that hangs between us, faded almost like the color of a bruise. And the light extends and stretches thin across the dark of yard.

It's somewhere here, while staring at this window, that M finally tells me where she got the joint. From a friend of a friend (of a friend). Some guy, she says, she doesn't really know, named Stoney. We'd already smoked the whole thing when she tells me this, and, at the name, with our eyes squinting sharp, with our mouths lifted at their corners, we laugh ourselves to quiet—to the movement of the neighbors' family dog two houses down and all the crickets in the grass and the solitary owl that hints its caution somewhere far beyond us and this place.

And anyway, I don't speak up about it right away: about my tongue and then the back wall of my throat—and how my body's growing, slowly, numb.

Imagine, M says to me, that window. *If she only knew what we were doing.*

Our grandmother, she means.

And that square of light: it feels both permanent and not. I swallow, and I swallow—moths flicker—and I swallow. I swallow, and I swallow.

She'd die, M says. *She'd be on the floor, like*—she snaps her fingers—*that.*

We both laugh something quick again, and quiet—again. I shake my head.

You know as well as we do that M has a point. I can't help but think about our grandmother's shame, and the way that shame requires performance. Or, rather, how shame, sometimes, *performs*: how, *if she only knew,* she might parade us to the front row of her church on Sunday—tomorrow morning, even—and make us ask forgiveness. Make us fall to knees in front of everyone. And her congregation, those witnesses, they'd sing—they'd *sing,* and our grandmother, the soprano, her voice would rise and shake above the rest until we're crying—maybe, *sobbing*—not because we feel convicted, or because we feel as if we're changed or led to change, but because no one can outlast, outrun, the weight of shame. Not forever. Not without some break, or some return.

I'm sure that *if she only knew,* she'd die of shame, and we might too. In some way.

So, we stare at the window. We keep our voices low. And soon, the window's light goes out.

Everything, for a moment, goes dark.

My heartbeat feels a half-beat off when M turns to me. There's a breeze that rustles windchimes, and she pulls the blanket draped across her legs to just below her chin. She asks me how I'm feeling. And I don't know, really, what to tell her. The truth is, at this point, my mouth feels like the dentist. And the feeling in my tongue's gone, near completely. And I can't feel the back of my throat, and there's a growing tingle in my legs. And yes: I'm scared we'll be found out.

I tell her that I'm feeling fine. I try a smile. Why?

She looks at me. I can't make out the color of her eyes, anything. *Are you?* she asks.

I mean, I start. I pause. I *guess* I am.

You guess?

My tongue, I say. And, I don't know. My tongue feels kind of weird.

Weird?

I nod. A little numb, I say, but the statement comes out almost like a question.

She bites her lip again. I notice a tilt in her voice, a shake. *Yeah,* she says, and, *same.*

Dog, crickets, owl.

I ask her if she wants to go inside. My tongue's a weight inside my mouth. My heart is pounding, and something in my head, behind my eyes, is clawing to get out. It's getting cold.

Back in the SHACK, M layers blankets over the sheets of the bed and crawls beneath them like escape. I close the door and turn the lock. I layer blankets on myself, and we both lie there, side by side and back to silence. There's so much silence, I think, some *distance,* between us and this and everything these days, and I stare up at the ceiling as she's staring at her phone. I feel that heartbeat kicking its wild rebellion in me, like it just might get away if I don't—breathe—and I feel cold, like my body's still outside, and all my breath feels heavy, textured, before I start to shake. All this, to myself.

All this to *myself,* I think, because I'm the older brother. First-born son. Because someone in this family has to level-out, stay calm.

And M turns her phone to me. And she shows me what she's doing. In the search bar: *tongue numb smoking.* The description beneath the purple link: words like *laced with* and *mosquito spray.*

I think, she says, a shake in her voice, *there might've been something in that joint.*

Stoney, I think. A friend of a friend (of a friend).

And I remember—or I think that I remember—how the joint had tasted *bitter.* Off.

I roll my eyes. You shouldn't Google that, I say. You shouldn't Google *any*thing right now.

That stuff will only make you paranoid, I tell her.

But *mosquitospraymosquitospraymosquitospray* is all that I can think.

OKAY, SO, I'll admit: maybe we're just stoned. Too stoned. *Way* too stoned. Maybe this, like everything, will pass, and this rambling's really all for nothing. But it's a weird thing, to think you're dying. And in your grandparents' backyard guesthouse. The LOVE SHACK. (Jesus.) I begin to wonder about next moves: on walking slow up to the house and through the sliding door. Silent, down the hallway, past the bedroom where your girlfriend lies asleep, and at the hallway's end: the *green room,* what we call it—because of all the pillows and the blankets and the wallpaper—where, at this moment, you must be sleeping too. I wonder how to knock, to wake you. How to walk in, or to stand in the doorway, your child, an adult, to tell you that I'm worried. Scared. That I've done something that I shouldn't have, and that I might need help. To calm my heart. This shaking. I wonder at your waking up, and if it'd be like childhood: how your body might lift onto an elbow, blinking, waking, in the dark; how a low, confused, and helpless single question might escape you:

You okay?

I imagine, too, worst-case scenarios: the red and blue lights, flashing, off of every neighbor's home. The reflection in every pane of glass holding this domestic shake-up: the wheeling-out of our bodies, already dead, maybe, or hanging on, and neighbors crawling out of front doors and spilling into yards like animals in spring to stand with hands held over open mouths that yawn or freeze in shock. They clutch the strings of bathrobes to themselves or run back in for slippers, blankets, whatever to keep warm. *How sad,* they'll say to one another. *How terrible.* How embarrassing. They'll talk about it all for weeks, at school and at the grocery store, *Those Mason grandkids,* and they'll shake their heads. How sad, indeed. How terrible, my god. I imagine how you'll run back in for car keys, a change of clothes, or, if there's nothing to be done, how you'll arch your body near the bushes of the front yard like you're looking for something, something that's been dropped. The woman that might be your future wife will stand beside you, rubbing at your neck, or else stand staring out a window with a tissue in her hand. I imagine how our grandfather might stand, too, with his hands pressed down into pajama-bottoms or with one palm pressed against your back. He'll squint because it's late, because he left his glasses on the nightstand. He'll turn his head to follow all that's left of that scene: the wailing of the EMT, its lights fading up the street. The wailing of our grandmother—

DO YOU remember, Dad, that hotel room in Dallas? The details aren't so clear, but I remember this: the three of you—we're still a family then—have come to visit me at college. You and I sit, waiting. Ready, I think (I don't remember), for dinner. You're sitting on a patterned couch, and I'm sitting in a patterned chair, and we're both watching something on TV. A movie, TNT or AMC, most likely, loud and full of action, though the volume's turned way down. We can hear the sounds of hairspray through the closed door to the bedroom and the wet puff of an iron steaming on a board. We can hear my mother and my sister pacing from the clothes they've both laid-out on beds to their reflections in the bathroom mirror. They talk, but it's like some distant rumbling through the walls. The message isn't clear. Their words, like this memory: held back. Restrained.

I'm 19, then. It'd been a year, at least, by that point—nearing two—since I came out to you.

It'd seemed, at first, and for a long time, like you might never talk again. So, I'm not so sure how we both got there: that time alone. All I know is, by then, I'd given up or given over to this new father: the one who ran on daylight and who closed his eyes as soon as it got dark. Who orbited the house on weekends like a planet of his own, finding ways to fill up space and time or fix it. This new father didn't speak a word at dinner. No longer asked about our days at school or work but asked Our God to bless the food and family. His look held resignation, and his gaze held to the floor.

Your father, my mother had said around that time, and paused—and I think, now, that, then, she'd already given up on you, had already made her mind up, maybe, moved on, and well before the rest of us could ever really know. *He's just,* she had said, *not changing.*

On your position. Where you stood. Acceptance. Your gay son, my coming out.

We'd gone downstairs to wait while the other two got finished. In my memory, light floods in like cool water from the windows up along the high ceiling so that the lobby's bathed near silver with it. There's an empty bar with empty tables—save one, save us— and a shallow pool and running river split the room in half. In the pool, two swans swim lazy circles, silent. Beneath their kicking feet lie dull and shining pennies that cover up the deep blue tile. There's a sign, too, beside the water, with their picture on its surface, and a description: where they came from, how they've come to this. Occasionally, one swan breaks free, away from the other, and follows the minor river's path: beneath a bridge and toward a waterfall. But it always turns around, and I watch its drifting back.

I stare, silent, at those birds. Their progress. Their narrow path, that closed circuit. I know I must feel sad that what I'm seeing is their life—just an aimless wandering around the same old things, unchanging—but I probably hold this in because you're looking off to somewhere else. Because we don't talk about the things like that. And anyway, the bartender's walking back. He pulls a beer off his tray and sets it down in front of you. A soda down in front of me. Two white napkins, black straws, and then he walks away.

There's that silence—and it's our silence—and it's sustained.

And because we've held so long to silence, I don't know, then, how to respond when you turn to me and, finally, you say something: what I remember: and the swan, it turns to rush back home: *I'm sorry.*

IN THE SHACK, I say to M that maybe we should sleep. Maybe we'll wake up (full-stop), feeling better in the morning.

Maybe, I say, probably, we've gone *far* too far outside ourselves.

I stand up, feeling dizzy. I walk over to the light switch on the wall and click it off. The inside of the SHACK turns dark, but there's the shallow glow of a nightlight streaming out from the bathroom. Its minor hue tints blue the floor and walls and gives the room, I think—or I begin to think—a look like it's submerged. Like M and I have settled on an ocean floor. (Like childhood rooms.) Like maybe we're just feeling its compression, and we only need to hold on, float up—*wait*.

And it'd be here, I think, inside the blue-tint glow and at the closing of the letter that I'd leave for you to find: some final chance to tell you how, in case we're really dying, I can't stop thinking, now, about that hotel lobby. Your *I'm sorry*. And if that *sorry* sought to change us. If you could finally see the cracks, or if you finally thought to fix them. To reverse that change, closing in.

And then, I might admit: how I wish that someone—you— would tell me if that *sorry* was just some last attempt to save us. Not just you and me, but her: my mother, your wife. Our family.

And at this, I imagine that I'd start to feel lightheaded. More- so than before, outside, and I'd drop the pen and hold my hands above the paper, shaking. My heart, it might feel like a step away from going off. Blowing up or shutting down. It might feel like a turning over in its cage, and here, I'd press a hand to my chest and feel for trying breath, the beat that's slowing—down.

Before I'd take the pen again. Pick up where I left off: the impos- sible task of writing this, and I'd write it, loud, across the paper, in case you find us unresponsive in the morning: *I'm sorry too*.

I'm sorry that I ever started saying no to fishing or to camping, to cutting paths on unmarked trails and skipping stones and hik- ing. That we ever stopped leaving brand-new pennies under rocks to mark our time together, or carving the initials of our names, those early years, on fallen trees. That I'm too far away to hear your *ky-oats* singing anymore. Deer, screaming in the hills. I'm sorry that I still can't change the oil in my car. For all the times you lifted up the hood and wiped your hands with blue shop rags and bent inside and pointed. That this inability to change applies to tires, too, and batteries. To pool filters. To any great machine: those unhurried and, still, overworked extensions of yourself. I'm sorry that I felt—or, that *I feel*—sometimes I want to run away. From you and from our family, and from home, West Texas, God. From everything and nothing. To turn my back to where I came from, to shut out generations of the men *like men* that came before me. To get into my car and drive. I'm sorry that I'm not always what you think of as a man. That the shock of my sin came at you like a sudden flash in the dark. That things like understanding sin and loving it, or learning how, take time. I'm sorry that I could never say this all before. That I kept mostly silent with the swans, and then, again, on that November morning, when we were looking out from where you stopped us at the ruins of a home. When family stood up to the edge of both our thinking. When there was no sound but the engine. But most of all, and just in case this really is the end:

I'm sorry that I feel, somehow, responsible for all of this.

IV

CODA

He sits alone. His truck hums in the quiet.

Let's say, Reader, that it's a park.

Outside the windshield caked with dirt, great clustered oaks stand veiled in shadow. Pale beams of light shoot down from up above them, shoot through their tangled tops, and mark the old park's miles of winding trails of sidewalk. Swings shake to the warm midsummer Texas breeze and falter to a still when that half-a-breeze dies down. The truck's light aims and tapers off to pierce its double dull reflections in the nearby slide; against the fire pole; to glow inside the eyes of one of several gathered spring-horses: one whose black mane grows in plastic, faded, now, from years of dry heat and the sun. And the spring-horse looks like it might smile—or that it might have, once.

He sits inside. Not going anywhere but waiting. Staring, out the window. Picking, anxious, at the right thigh of his jeans. We wonder how he spends his time in silence. How loud he's got the radio. How quiet. Let's say that it's turned up, but just enough: enough to wonder what the song is; to wonder what it is that comes on at this hour, well past sunset. If it's something country, slow, and classic. If they're lyrics from his youth. If he sings those lyrics under breath and keeps on looking at the time. In the rearview, in the mirrors on either door. Back ahead of him. Let's imagine that he must: that he sings: that the words come out deep and twangy, sad, like well-known hymns. That, like his song, the dark inside the truck is deep. Enough so that the orange and green and yellow dashboard tones blend and cling light shadow to the features of his face. That the center console, too, gives off a light that's bright enough to read that face, and still, that's low enough to hide it.

His face: those eyes that look, always, like crying but that can't. That don't, not now. Not yet. That mouth that's always working, always shaping lines and circles in between his speaking. That hangs open, sometimes, slight, in concentration. And it's hard to see—his mouth, beneath that new and untrimmed mustache. The same sandy color of his hair, graying where the rest of him is not. We wonder if the mustache makes him feel younger, or outside of himself, somehow. If it marks, to him, the present age: this present chapter: this new man, still in silence.

And he watches her pull up. And her headlights graze the swing; the slide; the fire pole and spring-horse. They hold onto something, those lights—or we imagine that they must: two strangers on that trail ahead, far and walking farther. Away from the red truck's humming in the parking lot. These strangers, they hold hands. They walk against the tree line, dip into it. Disappear. And when she steps out from a car no longer running, the strangers, then, are gone and swallowed by the dark.

We imagine that she knocks before she enters. On the passenger door. Or its window.

We imagine that she doesn't knock. That, instead, she swings the red door open on her own to make a light pop on inside the truck that holds her figure in the dark. And he reaches for the radio. And he turns it down, or off, because she's standing there, outside—and he feels he needs to focus. To steady himself. So he reaches for the steering wheel, and he grips it, like a natural reaction.

We wonder, then, how long it is she stands there.

How long the light holds, if it does.

Who speaks first. And what it is they say.

Let's say they don't say anything at all. That they only look at one another until the inside light clicks off and they're both bathed together in that strangers' dark, and she crawls, deep, into it.

Let's say it goes like this: that when she opens up the door, she laughs. That there's a sadness in it. That it's the first thing in almost two years that he hears from her—that he really hears at all. And when he asks her what's so funny, she tells him: *You,* she says. She taps her upper lip. *You have a mustache.* And he laughs, but his laughter catches. So that he has to look ahead. To the glowing eye of that old spring-horse, looking back. And she just shakes her head and stares down at the seat. Pale fabric, in this light. The breeze outside runs cool along her legs and rushes underneath the growling truck. And she holds on to the door, tight, with a sudden honest feeling like the whole thing—like this moment, he, she, and the truck—might lift off and float away, for good. Let's say that she believes it, because she keeps her tight hold on the red door when she looks back up to him. She stares until he meets her gaze. And together, for the time it takes to really look and see someone, the both of them forget to breathe. She lets out something like a sigh that's quick to leave before she bites her mouth.

Flares her nostrils. Feels the skin along her forehead crease. Her mouth, her body, shakes, and there's a silence, then, let's say, that settles in: that's full of all the things they want to say.

So many things, the other thinks, *but how the hell to say them?*

So she reaches for the handle just above the seat and pulls herself inside. She reaches for the door and pulls it toward herself to slam so they're alone. And the radio, it's on and it's a whisper. And the low, cool blow of the A/C presses to their skin and tremors every small hair lifting on their arms. And the light above them dims to dark—to stares forced to adjust, to the dashboard's glow.

He still thinks she's beautiful. Even more-so now—at almost 50. Her hair still settles just below her shoulders, and its color blends into the empty shade around them. She still catches it to hold behind her ears. Her eyes stare forward, off, and hard into the place in front of her like the airbag might release. Like she might will it to. And her hands—lotion-smooth—he sees they're starting, now, to wrinkle. They still rub rough with effort, one into the another, on and on.

What, she might say, then, *are we doing?* And she looks up to him. And the skin under her eyes is pink, is raw, he thinks, in this half-light. Like she's been crying. And she's crying now: her eyes, and then the space around them, shimmer.

He sniffs. He waits to speak, because he can't.

She can smell his breath. His clothes, like several beers. The inside of the truck holds onto it.

Are you happy? he asks. After him, he means. It must hang for a moment. Above all sound.

Until she breathes in through her mouth and lets the breath leave with her answer.

With the radio. With a siren, closing distance. With the cry of that old home's train, its every hour yearning.

And he turns to her and says, *I'm sorry.* That things turned out—he doesn't say—like this.

You were so in love with me, she says, *and I—* But then, we think, she stops herself. She shakes her head. And this, her body's motion, looks just out of her control. And she finds her breathing's rhythm, and she falls back into it.

There's a pause that lingers. That's filled, then, with the sound of just their breathing.

And he says her name. *I still am.* And he lets himself—finally—let go. To feel everything, for a moment, and everything escapes him. He says her name again, and then, *I'm still in love with you.* And when he says her name a third time, the sound of it, we think, is like worship. Like a conjuring. A thing, he worries, that, left out of conversation, might hurry up her leaving him again.

Let's say she already knows that he still loves her. That she still loves him too.

But I can't, he says and keeps on saying it. Now that he's getting married, soon, to someone else. *I can't,* he says and shakes his head. Now that she's on the tail-end of that other man's divorce. The man she left him for. And he looks out through that dirtied windshield for the black eye of the spring-horse. And she looks for it, too, and presses down a hand against her chest. Where she expects the sting of something stalling—but it's a beat, she finds, that's always moving on.

And they see the strangers, up ahead, step back out from the tree line. Back into the light.

And they sit alone, together. And the truck hums just above their quiet.

Let's say that it's a park: where my mother and my father keep the engine running.

ACKNOWLEDGMENTS

I've been writing stories all my life, which isn't so unusual; I think most of us, in our own ways, do. (My mother has the earliest of mine laminated in a chest somewhere; something about a Super Dog and Super Cat—and other Super Animals, all dressed a little too like Superman—fighting crime between construction paper covers. Orange and pink and blue, if I remember right.) Though the content of my storytelling's changed a bit (maybe one day I'll go back to talking dogs and cats), support has, in some form, always been a constant. I've carried the stories in this collection with me for some time now, I've finally put them down; but it's taken a lifetime of those countless others to twist them into shape.

And, God, how lucky I've been:

To Jill Talbot, who saw it first. Who knows, and understands, the beauty of West Texas. Without her every hour spent with my words, her friendly push to always queer it up, her classroom inspiration—without the undergrad workshop that had me running to a genre that, so suddenly, felt *right*: the Essay—this book would never be. Thank you.

To Scott Blackwood and Corey Marks, who read *this* when it was *that*. Their kind attention to the manuscript, and their sharp insights and lines of questioning, helped tremendously in preparing me to better see and talk about the aim of the collection in ways that would have otherwise been (I know) impossible. Thank you too.

To the other English teachers of my life—the Ashleys and the Griffins and the Kings—for showing me how best to tend to language. How to nurture it, on and off the page. And how to pass this love along, a task that Salinger called one *beautiful, reciprocal arrangement*. Thank you, endlessly, for giving me the tools.

To Kristen Elias Rowley and her team at The Ohio State University Press—to Mad Creek Books, and to David Lazar and Patrick Madden for a place in the 21st Century Essays series—thank you for reading then believing in this work of mine. For bringing it (a dream) to life. I'm proud it's found its home with you.

To my workshop cohorts, who helped to make these pieces so much better than they were. To my closest friends, who never knew they did. Every 2AM slurred backyard conversation, every no-sleep (gaming, movie) marathon, every slow, cool nighttime drive—windows down and music up around the lake, the park, the neighborhood—has all been therapy to me. (Sometimes, this is writing.) Here's to more and more of that and those.

And to family. To Mams and Papa John, to Mim and Grandaddy. To the many cousins, aunts, and uncles whose love has formed me—wished or willed or accidentally—into this unsteady thing they call a *writer*: thank you for this life, and for the fuel.

To Mom. To Dad. To M. This is, and always will be, a love letter to *us* first.

(Moon and back again.)

21st CENTURY ESSAYS
DAVID LAZAR AND PATRICK MADDEN, SERIES EDITORS

This series from Mad Creek Books is a vehicle to discover, publish, and promote some of the most daring, ingenious, and artistic nonfiction. This is the first and only major series that announces its focus on the essay—a genre whose plasticity, timelessness, popularity, and centrality to nonfiction writing make it especially important in the field of nonfiction literature. In addition to publishing the most interesting and innovative books of essays by American writers, the series publishes extraordinary international essayists and reprint works by neglected or forgotten essayists, voices that deserve to be heard, revived, and reprised. The series is a major addition to the possibilities of contemporary literary nonfiction, focusing on that central, frequently chimerical, and invariably supple form: The Essay.

---

*Annual Gournay Prize Winner